# RENAISSANCE
## EUROPE
### 1480–1520

D0696133

J. R. HALE

# RENAISSANCE EUROPE
# 1480–1520

*Collins*

THE FONTANA HISTORY
OF EUROPE

# CONTENTS

# PREFACE

This book is planned on somewhat different lines from its companions in the Fontana History of Europe. While not ignoring the events on which a sense of chronology depends, it aims chiefly at providing a means of understanding the quality of the lives of as many people as the nature of the surviving evidence and the limitations of my own knowledge make possible. It is concerned with material circumstance but also with states of mind, not only to record what happened in the forty years from 1480 to 1520 but, and with greater emphasis, to suggest what it was like to have lived then.

Each chapter is designed to provide information about a specific field of inquiry and at the same time to offer an answer to certain basic questions that must be asked in order to understand men of any period. What were their feelings about the passage of time and about their environment? What sort of polity did they live within and what sense of relationship did they have with it and with other communities ranging in size all the way from the family to Christendom? Within what general economic framework and in what ways did they earn a living? How did they regard themselves and others in terms of status, occupation and living standards? What part did religion play in their lives, and what cultural and intellectual satisfactions were open to them?

I hope I am sufficiently aware of the danger of pretension which hangs over such an approach. But there are other hazards to which the reader should be alert. The evidence from which 'states of mind' at this period can be reconstructed is patchy and extremely difficult to assess; decisions about what evidence to use as well as what areas of experience to explore are ominously subjective. The desire to appraise the feelings of

possible to compare our own attitudes to questions of basic concern (social justice, say, or love, or the response to works of art) with those of past ages, and, vice versa, to review past attitudes in order to wonder afresh about our own.

This, at least, has been my experience as a teacher of Renaissance history here and in the United States, and my first acknowledgement of indebtedness is to my students at Warwick and Berkeley. I also owe a great deal to the encouragement of Professor G. R. Potter, who read the hideous bulk of the first draft as well as the proofs, to the firm and sympathetic guidance I received from Professor J. H. Plumb and to the detailed advice as well as the exemplary patience of Mr. Richard Ollard.

# CHAPTER I

# TIME AND SPACE

i

'O slow-moving clock', exclaimed the infatuated hero of Fernando de Rojas's romance *La Celestina*, 'would I could see you burned with the sharp fires of love! If you expected the same joys as I at midnight, you would cease to obey the will of the craftsman who made you ... But what am I demanding? ... There is a fixed period for the secret revolutions of the celestial firmament, the planets and the north star, and for the monthly waxing and waning of the moon ... What would it profit me that my iron clock struck twelve, if the heavenly clock did not agree?'*

This comparison of clock time with natural time was no mere trope. Though clocks had long ceased to be a novelty, for most men time meant the length of a task within the context of sunlight and season. Nature set the alarm and measured the day. 'At dawn', 'about noon', 'towards sunset': these were still the commonest references to time. The month was seen in terms of its characteristic rural activity within a calendar of survival. Emotionally, the year began with the first flowers, the lengthening of the day, the first judgement on the fortune of the winter-sown grain. Only those concerned with legal or diplomatic documents thought of the year as beginning on an official rather than a seasonal date, and even here there was no uniformity, the date on which a new year started varying, country by country, from December 25th to January 1st, March 1st, March 25th and September 1st. It could vary in this way from city to city and even for different types of documents within one city: in Rome bulls were dated according to

* Here, as elsewhere, I quote from the translation by C. M. Cohen, *The Spanish Bawd* (London, 1964).

After their slow introduction from the fourteenth century, clocks were striking the hours in towns all over Europe. The system of counting them, however, differed. In Italy clocks struck from 1 to 24 starting at sunset, in Germany from 1 to 24 starting at sunrise, in England and Flanders from 1 to 12 starting at midday and midnight. Every town had its own time based on the moment when the sun dipped behind, or rose above its own particular local horizon. Though many clocks struck the hour, fewer had a minute hand, very few indeed struck the quarters. And all were inaccurate and required frequent resetting. Though the clock with its equal hours did help to introduce a different concept of time, we must not see the contrast in terms of the conflict between the times of the sun and of the machine, the 'natural' tempo of the countryside and the 'unnatural' one of the town, that characterised the Industrial Revolution. Many small villages in France and the Low Countries possessed public clocks. A petition of 1481 urging the town council of Lyons to install 'a great clock whose strokes could be heard by all citizens in all parts of the town', pointed out that 'if such a clock were to be made, more merchants would come to the fair', but other reasons too were offered: 'the citizens would be very consoled, cheerful and happy and would live a more orderly life and the town would gain in decoration'. Moreover, certain routines, like the changing of the watch in garrison towns, the closing of city gates for the night and the establishment of a curfew hour after which crimes were punished by a double or even a quadruple penalty, called for accurate time-keeping. In the towns men made appointments and attended meetings: clocks expressed the social convenience of a common and precise vocabulary of time as well as an attitude to the spacing of the day in the interest of profit. The large public sundial set on the façade of a medieval church or city hall and the pocket dial: these had told the time almost as effectively, if with less insistence. The multiplying of clocks and the introduction at this time of portable clocks and spring-driven watches (even more inaccurate than town clocks) reflected fashion as well as need. Antonio de Beatis, who accompanied the cardinal of

40 years . . . Queriot Nichalet, butcher, age about 60 . . . Pernet Callet, labourer, age about 27, Colin Byson, householder, age about 80.' Yet for organisational purposes governments had to assume a precision that did not exist. When an army had to be raised, the ages for enlistment were carefully spelled out. The upper limit at which men were assumed to be fit for military service was commonly 60, the lower limit varied with the urgency of the situation from 20 to 15. For taxation purposes the lowest chargeable age was also spelled out, commonly as low as 15.

In Florence a man came politically of age at 14: at that age he could be summoned to attend a *parlamento*. There, as elsewhere, minimum age limits were set to appointments to the various organs of government, and to the period of reduced penalties 'propter aetatis imbecillitatem' in the administration of criminal law. Manuals for confessors named 14 as the age when a knowledge of the nature of mortal sin might be assumed. During the controversy about the forcible baptism of Jewish children, 12 was named as the minimum age at which this might be permitted. Legal majority differed from place to place but was always clearly defined, so was the age at which a young prince could dispense with a regency or at which a feudal dependant had to pay homage or a ward could resume his inheritance.

Yet even at these upper reaches of society uncertainty about age was common, especially outside Italy. One of the seamiest lawsuits of the age was the attempt of Charles VIII's successor, Louis XII of France, to obtain an annulment of his marriage so that he could marry Charles' widow Anne instead, thereby preventing her from withdrawing her duchy of Brittany from the jurisdiction of the French crown. Louis claimed, with the wealth of physical detail required to sustain his accusation of malformation, that he had been unable to have sexual relations with his wife. This was not only an unpleasant, but an uncertain charge. Jeanne was able to produce evidence to the contrary including witnesses who swore that the king had come in one morning saying, 'I have earned, and well earned a drink, for I mounted my wife three or four times dur-

ancients into the system of humours and accepted by the
medicine of the day: blood dominant from midnight to dawn,
choler from dawn to noon, melancholy from noon till dusk
and phlegm from dusk to midnight. Literature and sermon
gave wide currency to the notion that life was measured less
tellingly by years than by such stages as infancy, youth,
maturity, old age and senility: stages all the more dramatic
because malnutrition and disease compressed them into an
average life expectancy of some 30 to 35 years, and among
those who lived longer all but the rich began to take on the
physical attributes of old age. Erasmus (who lived to be about
70) recorded gloomily that at 35 dried-up old age tires the
body's strength. Priests found it difficult to obtain the services
of housekeepers who had attained the no longer scandal-
provoking age of 40. The Utopian people described in Antonio de Guevara's *Relox de Principes* (*c.* 1518) indeed, killed
all their women at 40 and their men at 50 to save them from
the weaknesses into which the aged lapsed.

Perhaps 50 per cent of children, and not only those of the
poor, died in their first year. No special regard for childhood
as a separate, precious state grew from this holocaust of infants. Children were dressed in adult styles and hurried into
adult occupations. They were subjected to no special discipline
nor were they insulated by nurseries and reticences from the
pre-occupations of adults. Schooling was not taken for granted,
it did not involve uniform or boarding or a special code of
behaviour; at universities students were largely self-governing;
no convention, but only circumstance, divided the carefree
from the responsible years. The 'five ages' owed their poign-
ancy to the fact that they were not related so closely to different moods and different sorts of activity as to the all-too-short
passage of man's body from one form of helplessness to another. Generational time was haunted by the image of decrepit
age, the crooked back and toothless grimace of a thousand
carvings and caricatures. In painting, engraving and woodcut
the legend of the Fountain of Life held out its illusory
promise; from all directions greybeards came hobbling to
drag themselves over its rim and tumble into its waters—

and poisoned the security of all; famines like those of 1502–3 and 1506–7 in Spain could depopulate whole regions whence the survivors, as a contemporary put it, 'wandered down the roads carrying their children, dead of hunger, on their backs'. The physical and nervous tone of life was conditioned by what men could afford to eat.

In many aspects of life, if only for a minority, this period was one of change, but diet constituted a drab and universal continuity with the middle ages. It was not only that food supplies were precarious, the possibility of starvation and the probability of a permanently enfeebling malnutrition omnipresent; at its best the diet of the majority was not calculated to build energy or preserve health but to produce the moods of nervy restlessness, the fits of panic that underlay some at least of the political discontent and the religious crazes of the time. Overwhelmingly it was a farinaceous diet: wheat, rye, barley, oats, millet; the commonest meal was bread floating in a thin vegetable soup. Fresh meat was eaten rarely, perhaps a dozen times a year by most families. Because of the concentration on cereals and the difficulty of keeping stock alive during the winter the animal population was small; butchers were only to be found in sizeable towns, their supplies were intermittent and their charges high. Milk and butter and the hard, keeping cheeses were all expensive and the poor townsmen probably never tasted them. Eggs and an occasional fowl provided the main variety in the country. A pig was more likely to be sent to town or the local manor for cash than eaten, because of the high cost of salting it. Game was jealously protected by the large landowners. Fresh sea fish was of course available only near the coast and it is doubtful whether salt fish played a part in the ordinary man's diet; the costs of salting and transport meant that he normally kept his Fridays and other fast days by not varying his normal meatless diet. Rivers and lakes were fished—on the town wall of Constance was a circle showing which fish was best to eat in each month of the year—but fishing rights were restricted to the big riparian landlords and much of the catch channelled to market or to monastic or noble households.

nearer than six hours to DINNER and to wear bracelets of lead so that his hands will not fly so readily to his mouth. DINNER escapes with a scolding, but BANQUET, having confessed the grossness of his conduct, is ceremoniously hung by DIET as a warning to the audience.

It was a warning that few needed to take to heart, but it was repeated by inference in the legislation by which governments attempted to limit the number of dishes that might be served at weddings and other occasions of rejoicing; the consumption of the well-to-do must not be such as to excite the jealousy of the poor. The printing of cookery books, of which the English *Boke of Kerving* (1508) is an early example, suggests that among the reasonably wealthy a more sophisticated mean was becoming established between fast and feast; if we wish, however, to understand the sense of time as it is marked off by red-letter days, we must imagine a calendar of widely spaced and memorable excesses at the table.

No topic figured more consistently in royal and municipal legislation than attempts to keep down the price of bread, to prevent the forestalling of grain and to encourage the movement of supplies to areas of dearth. Of all food markets that of grain was most commonly overlooked architecturally, as well as administratively, by the town hall; grain stores, from the heavily barred magazines of the north to the underground silos of the Mediterranean islands, were as important to the preservation of law and order within the city as were its walls to protection from without. The fields yielded poorly, seldom enough to provide plenty for all. The landlord and the church took their portion before distribution could begin; poultry and livestock absorbed another fraction before the grain could move (were a surplus left from local needs) to market and to brewery—for throughout northern Europe, grain for drink competed strongly with grain for food. Of all the food products discovered in the Americas before the later importation of the potato it was maize that was seized on with the greatest avidity; from its introduction *c*. 1500 it began to spread from Spain across France, Italy and the Balkans. That a balanced diet was known to be desirable is shown from the stores taken

tries without this subsidised and tradition-supported ritual the cost and inconvenience of heating water, and the high price of tallow- or olive oil-based soap meant that bodies went dirty to table and to bed. In some places it was the custom to wear a little piece of fur on the person as an encouragement to bugs to congregate there, in others mulberry twigs were put under the bed to divert the fleas: the wealthy Venetian Marco Falier noted in his household accounts in 1509 that he had renewed them at the cost of five *soldi*. Etiquette books reflected a growing concern for domestic hygiene: some were printed in verse to aid the memory, some were set to popular tunes, like the German *Tischzucht im Rosenton*. 'Your nose, your teeth, your nails from picking/Keep at your meat' advised an English work—and don't spit on the table.

When physicians were reduced to saying 'anyone who drinks half a spoonful of brandy every morning will never be ill' and housewives wisely preferred home-brewed elixirs to leech and lancet, it was the city fathers rather than the doctor who saved lives. Great care was taken, for example, that when meat was available it should not spread disease. The statutes (1514) of the butchers' guild of Chevreuse, a small town in the Île de France, specified, among other regulations, that any pig which had been reared on or near the premises of a barber's shop or smithy should be fed in a separate place for nine days (twenty, in the case of a hospital) before being killed. But no regulations were efficacious against plague. Houses were sealed off and identified with daubed crosses, the sale of infected clothing was forbidden, large bonfires were kept burning in every open space, sanitary inspectors searched for undisclosed sufferers, but nothing stopped the appearance of the blueish-black abscess in the arm-pit or the palm of the hand that was the herald of a few days of agony followed, probably in the majority of cases, by death. Venice, forced by constant commerce with the east to adopt the most stringent health regulations in Europe, was helpless before the plague; Titian's early masterpiece, St. Mark Enthroned, was painted as an *ex voto* after the plague of 1510 in which his young contemporary, Giorgione, died. In 1484 a schoolmaster in Deventer wrote to

did it spare the cultivated and wealthy. Konrad Celtis contracted it as early as 1496, his fellow humanist, Ulrich von
Huten, wrote a highly successful book about its cure but
nevertheless died of it, Erasmus himself was a sufferer and so
was Albert Dürer's friend and patron Willibald Pirckheimer.
The number of bishops named raises the suspicion of gossip,
but there is some cause to believe that Pope Julius II was
syphilitic, even if this did little to daunt his heroic constitution.
The disease, in fact, maimed far more victims than it killed,
but its repulsiveness and the pain it caused sustained the
horror that was felt.

Doctors were not slow to produce reasons, mainly astrological, for the outbreak of the scourge, together with remedies,
though the first marginally effective one, the taking of mercury
internally, was not proposed until 1512. Meanwhile public
authorities took panic measures. In 1497 James IV of Scotland
ordered all syphilitics into isolation on an island in the Firth
of Forth. In Paris, early in the same year, notice was given by
handbell throughout the streets that all infected residents were
to repair to improvised quarantine quarters at S. Germain-des-
Pres; all infected non-residents were to leave within 24 hours
through two named gates where they were to sign for transport
money and proceed at once to their homes. All this on pain of
death. Such measures were too drastic to be taken seriously
and the disease raged on through Europe as it was to rage
through Polynesia some three centuries later. The German
emperor Maximilian used syphilis as a sign that God, as the
mystic year 1500 approached, was scourging mankind, and he
urged his people to shun their evil ways and join the crusade
he was attempting to raise against the Turks.

iii

To the uncertainty brought by disease to a man's estimate of
his probable life span, violence, organised or casual, added
another troubling dimension. The wars of this period were
fought with far larger armies than had been raised hitherto

sort in Bayonne in 1488, and in Montauban and Moissac in 1493. In 1500 the streets of Paris were overrun by men threatening to throw grain merchants into the Seine. There were food riots at Nevers in 1507. At Agen in 1514 the mob took complete charge of the town and, before the military could close in, clamoured for the equal distribution of goods and the exclusion of the rich from municipal government. With Lyons on the verge of a similar explosion in 1515, the magistrates forbad public meetings and censored all popular entertainments in case they contained egalitarian propaganda; two years later the city was given over to armed bands of artisans. It was small wonder that the carrying of weapons was prohibited and a curfew imposed on the streets at night in most European towns; any man abroad after dark had to carry a torch and explain his purpose to the watch, and frequently streets were fitted with chains that could be unwound from their drums and used to seal them off on any suspicion of trouble.

Considerable space was given in manuals of advice for confessors to the need to persuade parishioners to keep the peace; not to provoke others to quarrels, not to incite neighbours by noise or challenging gestures or by malicious gossip. Gambling was deplored as the age's commonest cause of affrays. Governments forbad it in taverns, captains on ships, gild statutes among apprentices—and vainly. This was class legislation. Henry VIII could lay his bets on chess, dice, cards, archery or tennis in the full light of court, the wager book of the Hansa merchants in Danzig shows them betting on the duration of a war, the results of an election or a tournament, on the price of herring, on the chances of a cook pointing to her landlord as the most probable father of her children; they could afford to lose. It was above all the poor man who was quick to feel himself cheated and reach for his knife, especially after drinking; court records are filled with tavern savagery and small brutal peasant vendettas. But there was an undercurrent of violence in all levels of society. It was present even in their pastimes. Jousts were expected to produce casualties. It was common for the mock-battles staged as pageants to become real

coming notably milder. Throughout western Europe the criminal law, when public order was not concerned, was un-fairly summary in its processes but not savage. Practice varied from country to country—tongues were ripped out in Italy for a blasphemous swearing bout which in France would cost seventeen sous, and the law could easily be stampeded into panic violence, but the average man was not ill-protected; it was the powerful subject who might expect the complete arbitrariness which is the scapegoat's fate, from Henry VIII's propaganda killing of his father's unpopular financial agents Empson and Dudley to Machiavelli's object lesson, the politic assassination of Ramiro D'Orco as a sop to Cesare Borgia's Romagnol subjects. The enormous volume of litigation in spite of delays and high fees displays the law not only as a means of damping down violence but as an arena where com-bative instincts could seek a public, formalised and usually bloodless release.

The veneer placed over violence by the law, the Com-mandments and by reasonably prosperous times was, however, thin and easily broken, especially when God's apparent deter-mination to scourge his people led to waves of panic. To the scourge of plague was added that of the infidel. The horror spread by tales of Turkish atrocities during the occupation of Otranto in 1480 was expressed not only in print, but in paint-ing through a rash of Martyrdoms of the Holy Innocents. In 1496 a physician writing about syphilis was moved to ask not only whether the disease, as a punishment for sin, was beyond human cure but whether this was not true of all disease, a failure of nerve that underlay the growing—and novel—ten-dency to identify all mental illnesses with the operation of the devil and therefore with witchcraft. The millenarian death-wish of the middle ages, exacerbated for some by the approach of the year fifteen hundred, took on a deepened morbidity in the many versions of the *Life of Antichrist*: a Jew begets the Beast on his own daughter, amidst adoring sycophants it cir-cumcises itself and triumphs over those who deny him as they are sawn, burned, crucified or buried alive. As the end of the century approached, rumours and portents multiplied: mon-

Time past was being mastered. Historians could now look back in perspective. Episodes which frequently had hovered timelessly in the medieval chronicle were now commonly located with reference to a chronological vanishing point. Historical characters seen in terms of a fairly realistic psychology became easier to imagine and identify with. A search for causation which explained events in terms of human weaknesses and ambition strengthened the narrative thread of history, and some discrimination in the use of sources enhanced its intellectual appeal. For information, patriotic reassurance, in search of wisdom or an enhanced sense of personal identity, or purely for escape, men entered this organised past in increasing numbers. Edition followed edition of Livy, Caesar, Josephus, Eusebius and Valerius Maximus (to take a sample from one printing centre, Lyons), medieval chronicles were revised and new ones issued in response to a demand from the whole reading public. For time to come, on the other hand, there were no guide lines save those, potentially ominous, projected forward by the church. There was no concept of secular progress save in the sense of a more effective recovery of the past: the consolation of ancient wisdom, the spur to emulate ancient achievements. There was no notion that man could improve his physical lot, that food could be increased, disease routed, life made more convenient or comfortable. Both the humanitarian and the technological motives for planning hopefully for the future were lacking. For the vast majority the future was not a zone where a man could project with some confidence his own achievements and those of his posterity nor speculate optimistically about society as a whole: it was filled by the image of death.


iv


The sense of time is partly objective, influenced by calendars, tasks and clocks, partly subjective, affected by seasons, hunger and the individual's attitude to the stages of life and to his life expectation, and it is intellectually conditioned by the ability

groups, their clustered monuments and the patronage they extended to literature and the arts that drew the restless and the work-hungry along the roads and rivers of Europe to settle amidst new impressions or to collect them and pass on. For most of the men who enlarged their spatial horizon by travel it was a town that drew them to make the first move.

Hardship for the traveller was inevitable, and hazards great. The Venetian government, which had the most elaborate diplomatic network in Europe, had to impose heavy penalties to keep its agents on the move. In 1506, Francesco Morosini wrote from Turin to say that in crossing the Alps on his return from France several of his suite had died in snowstorms. Next year the papal legate returning from the meeting between Louis XII and Ferdinand of Aragon at Savona wrote that he had been sea sick 'usque ad sanguinem' and, indeed, he got back to Rome so weak that he contracted a fever and died. Diplomatic correspondence is full of horror stories and complaints about bad inns, rotten food, surly muleteers and (there was no waterproof clothing and the roads were too rutted for heavy closed carriages) constant exposure to wind and rain. The ambassadorial life was an alternation between ceremony and discomfort. There was, too, especially in the unpeopled spaces of eastern Europe, the constant fear of bandits. Even in the west travellers who were not rich enough to travel with a small cavalcade waited for a merchant convoy before passing through the more desolate regions.

Such regions were plentiful, as a glance at population figures, in rounded millions, will make clear: Germany, 20; France, 19; Russia (very uncertain), 9; Poland, 9; Castile, 6–7; the Balkans, south of the rivers Save and Danube, 5½; Burgundy (including Artois, Flanders and Brabant), 6; England, 3; the kingdom of Naples, 2; the Papal States, 2; Portugal, 1; Aragon, 1; Sweden and Switzerland, both ¾. People, then, were thin on the ground. There was a tendency for large town to become larger rather than for small ones to grow, or for villages to become towns. The traveller could have days of open country separating him from one oasis of comfort and another. Naples was an extreme case; with a population of well

the tax returns from which they can be compiled are often incomplete—or incompletely understood. But, from the point of view of the traveller, the picture is clear. Plotted on a map, the large, the safe, the hospitable towns amount to a few widely scattered dots. Only on the chief trade routes were inns to be found at intervals of ten to fifteen miles. Only the rich could afford to take enough food, bedding and armed men to diverge from the main routes. But though travel had its difficulties, anyone who wanted to move, could, and at speeds which hardly varied until the coming of the railways. From Paris to Calais, for instance, took $4\frac{1}{2}$ days, to Brussels $5\frac{1}{2}$, to Metz 6, to Bordeaux 7, to Toulouse 8–10, to Marseilles 10–14 and to Turin 10–15. From Venice it took Philippe de Commines 6 days to reach Asti, 'for the road was the best in the world'. Other average times from Venice were to Rome 4 days (though there is a record of a courier doing it non-stop in a day and a half), to London 26, to Madrid 42, to Constantinople 41. These are times taken by merchants or diplomats in a hurry. Along routes where there was an organised postal service the times could be still further clipped. In 1516 letters sent from Brussels via the postal system operated by the Taxis family reached Paris in summer in 36 hours, Lyons in $3\frac{1}{2}$ days and Rome in $10\frac{1}{2}$ days. Once off the main routes, however, and above all if a sea passage were involved, the times were impossible to forecast with any degree of accuracy.

The heaviest traffic consisted of traders, their goods and their agents, the traffic being at its height at the four seasonal fairs held at Lyons where, for a fortnight of intense activity, merchants brought samples from all over western Europe. Good roads, navigable rivers, a central position and royal protection made Lyons at these times the busiest of European cities. The city was also thronged by the stewards of wealthy families who travelled far to load a mule train with exotic supplies. The account books of one such purchaser, the agent of Princess Philiberta of Luxembourg, show how widely the net of commerce was cast. His purchases included spices from Venice, wine from Crete, currants from Corinth, salt fish from

fession, as was proof-reading. We hear much of itinerant bands of actors, jugglers and musicians, something of itinerant professional football and tennis players but almost nothing, alas, about the most symbolic wanderers of all, the gypsies. Treated most tolerantly in Scotland and Scandinavia, they were expelled from Spain (by law if not in fact) in 1499, from Burgundy in 1515; they were harassed elsewhere. That in spite of this they flourished, the widespread influence of their music shows, and from time to time the picture lightens; a gypsy band played at the wedding of Matthias Corvinus and Beatrice of Aragon in Buda in 1476 and they were mentioned as playing at court in 1483. On Corfu, under Venetian protection, a hundred gypsies formed a community exempt from galley service and the usual peasant labour services.

Wanderers almost as compulsive were students and scholars. Degrees could be built up piecemeal by residence at one university after another; for each student there was an ideal curriculum available, based on books by and hearsay about famous teachers, to be followed by moving not from one lecture hall but from one country to another. The study of Latin, Greek and Hebrew had produced a new and revolutionary mood in scholarship, both secular and Christian, and to take advantage of it scholars had to hurry from one spring to another as it bubbled through the rocks of traditional scholastic learning: to confer with colleagues, to exploit an eager publisher, to settle for a while under the wing of a sympathetic patron. To this end, More wrote in defence of his friend's restless itinerancy, 'Erasmus defies stormy seas and savage skies and the scourges of land travel' and goes 'through dense forest and wild woodland, over rugged hilltops and steep mountains, along roads beset with bandits ... tattered by the winds, spattered with mud, travel-weary.' But he does this both to learn and to give, for 'as the sun spreads its rays, so wherever Erasmus is he spreads his wonderful riches'.

This defence of one man's migrancy can serve for European culture as a whole, which was marked in this period by an unprecedented speed in the internationalisation of styles—or, rather, by an unprecedented exposure of national or local

Dionisio Memmo, was called from S. Marco to London in 1516. While the flow of executants tended to be from south to north, and led to a marginal import of musical fashions— Henry VIII danced in the first Italianate masque in 1513—the flow of composers and teachers was from north to south. The Englishman John Hothby (d. 1487) taught for twenty years in Lucca, but the majority originated in northern France and the Low Countries and spread the brilliant achievements of this area all over Europe. Johannes Tinctoris spent over twenty years (1474–95) at the Neapolitan court, where he demon- strated in practice, and through a number of treatises, the qualities of one of the period's most illustrious composers, Johannes Okegham. Okgeham himself spent some time in Spain under Ferdinand, and his northern influence was con- firmed when in 1516 Ferdinand's successor Charles brought with him a whole choir from the Netherlands.

Josquin des Prez, *doyen* of the composers of the period, was also a migrant from his home in Hainault; he worked in Milan, in the papal chapel in Rome and, at the turn of the century, at the court of Ercole d'Este in Ferrara. Thereafter he spent most of his time in France, dying there in 1521. These travels, plus the amiable practice whereby princes took their musicians about with them or lent performers to one another, meant that Europe learned, with remarkable speed, and by a process that happily reversed Gresham's Law, to speak a common musical language.

Administrative routines also drew many men away from their homes. Jury service, membership of a representative assembly, the need to plead at a superior court of law; these dislodged men, if infrequently and reluctantly, from an other- wise static existence and in a manner that was socially selec- tive, for the richer or better born a man was, the more likely that in both church and state he would be expected to travel to the central tribunals of the nation. This trickle of repre- sentatives, litigants or petitioners to the centre was paralleled by a movement of officials—judges, financial agents, royal messengers, commissions of inquiry—from the centre to the periphery.

with my own eyes'; that made Lodovico Varthema show 'the same desire to behold the various kingdoms of the world which has urged on others' so that in 1502, 'longing for novelty' he set off for Mecca disguised as a Moslem pilgrim and went on to trade with some success in Burma and Ceylon.

v

Travel does not, by itself, condition the sense of space. It depends upon the individual's reactions to the scenes through which he passes, and here there is a formidable problem of evidence. Were it not for the independent record of Dürer's watercolour sketches of landscape, for example, his travel diaries would suggest that he was interested in little more than the number of miles travelled, the people he met and the prices at inns.

Much of nature was, in any case, marked off from a tranquil appreciation of it for its own sake. Apart from infrequent and widely-scattered communities of fishermen and isolated bands of salt evaporators, the sea coast of Europe was deserted, its rocks and marshes a *cordon sanitaire* the traveller or trader only penetrated to embark or disembark. Even maritime countries like Portugal and Venice suffered from a shortage of sailors; a poor living scratched from the soil was more attractive than life on shipboard. No holiday-maker sought the sea. It was dangerous, a wreckers' world, unwritten about save in tones of dismay, unpainted save as the background to a miracle or a foreground to the welcoming quays of town. Mountains too were zones of fear and could be admired—save by a stratigrapher like Leonardo—only if their pastures and hanging woods enabled them to be seen as useful to man. The forests which covered so much of Europe were rarely penetrated save by huntsmen and fugitives from justice.

Appreciation of nature was also limited by dusk. Fear of the night was universal. There was no movement in or out of villages, cottagers barred their doors. If a neighbour screamed in the street, his cries went unheeded. Wolves roamed in the

laying the flower itself with what was often a strongly divergent image which had struggled through the middle ages unrefreshed by direct observations since the days of Dioscorides. Herbals and bestiaries showed common flowers and familiar animals in a convention that contradicted everyday experience, but these images had two sources of power: they symbolised knowledge and authority, and they were the accepted hieroglyphs which demonstrated the diverseness of God's creation and His direct concern for man. At the back of the eye which looked at nature was a pseudo-botany, a pseudo-zoology, and a pseudo-topography, for there were conventional symbols for tree and river and mountain; even when artists had demonstrated their ability to portray a city exactly, printers continued to illustrate verbal descriptions of different towns with the same conventionalised woodcut view. How far this inner vision affected ordinary vision it is, of course, impossible to say. There is a gap between the eye seeing and the pen or brush recording that we cannot measure, but we may guess that for most men it was filled by associations that obscured a straightforward 'love of nature'; utility, images from the pseudo-sciences, the sense of divine purpose in which love of nature became diffused into worship of God. From his villa at Poggio a Caiano, Lorenzo de' Medici could see that 'the olive on its gentle, open slope appears green or white according to the wind'. That is a flick of direct observation. In other poems by Lorenzo—in whom the feeling for nature was fresher than in almost any other writer of his age—the freshness is hardly more (and here he is more representative) than a scent clinging to motifs from medieval tapestries and classical literature: '*Cerchi chi vuol le pompe* . . . Let him who wants them seek pomp and honour, public squares, temples and grand buildings, pleasures and treasures which bring with them a thousand worries, a thousand pains. A green meadow full of lovely flowers, a stream which moistens the grass on its banks, a little bird that makes its plaint of love, these soothe our passions much better.'*

*Tr. Eve Borsook, *The Companion Guide to Florence* (1966) 244.

ence and which show the country as above all a place for love.
From homes where there was no privacy, from mattresses sour
with damp and hopping with fleas, the first warm days of
spring drew lovers to the fields and woods. Not without reason
are the age's two most tranquilly beautiful love scenes, the
*Mars and Venus* of Piero di Cosimo and Botticelli, placed in
the open air.

Art as a whole is a better guide than literature; while the
achievements of the ancients in landscape painting were known
from Pliny the Elder's descriptions of classical works there
were no surviving examples to copy or be influenced by. Technically, landscape had been rendered with considerable exact-
ness early in the fifteenth century; the river winding towards
hills in the background of Jan van Eyck's *Madonna of the
Chancellor Rolin* (1425) is a magnificent example. But in intention this is still nature as symbol. From about 1500 there
was a change away from using landscape as a symbol of the
creation or an allegory of a state of mind towards a feeling for
nature for its own sake, as the self-sufficient encloser of a mood,
not a finger post to some destination in the mind or soul.
Technical progress helped prepare the way for this change.
Mastery of compositional and aerial perspective meant that the
painter—a Dürer or a Giorgione—could come back from the
countryside with a whole landscape in his mind or in a sketch.
It enabled painters to use landscapes which had a personal
meaning for them so that they could record, easily and naturally, the setting of their own lives; thus the Arno valley was used
in Baldovinetti's *Nativity* and Pollaiuolo's *Martyrdom of S.
Sebastian*. These familiar backgrounds ceased to be symbols
because they were seen and recorded as a whole, as a scene,
not a working together of a river, a rocky hill, a forest, from
the iconographical dictionary every painter carried in his head.

The quality of feeling is not easy to assess, however. Did
Altdorfer dwarf the armoured saint in his *Forest with S.
George and the Dragon* with the overwhelming foliage of the
woods because he loved trees, or because they symbolised the
part of the country that was the special preserve of the knightly
class and their huntsmen? Indeed, did Pollaiuolo use the Arno

his teeth until he rejoins human society. Nature is something
to grumble at—too much pain, too cloudy, too cold, the sea
too rough—almost never to delight in: a vast unwelcome cor-
ridor connecting the warm halls of men. Even geographers and
topographers whose eyes were professionally open to new
scenes hardly ever express any feeling for them. Their concern was with place names, with productivity and with people;
the town where all accused persons were hung and dug up
and given Christian burial if they were subsequently proved
innocent—anthropological bizarreries of this kind were more
interesting than the landscape in which they were enacted.
Columbus alone of the explorers expressed a delight in nature,
but for all the nights he spent under tropical skies there is no
mention of the stars except as tricky things to navigate by, and
even his praise of landscape dwindled rapidly into utili-
tarianism: 'In that island Hispaniola there are mountains of
very great size and beauty, vast plains, groves and very fruit-
ful fields, admirably adapted for tillage, pasture and habita-
tion.'

## vi

It was above all a thoroughly practical search for useful products, especially gold and spices, that determined the sensation-
ally rapid opening of the aperture through which Europeans
could look at the world; the Cape of Good Hope rounded in
1488, the West Indies discovered in 1492, India reached by
sea in 1498, Brazil described in 1500, the Americas recognized
as a separate continent in 1513 when Balboa confirmed previous conjectures by sighting a 'new' ocean, the Pacific, South
America circumnavigated by Magellan in 1520.

These voyages, epoch-making as they were, were largely the
culmination of long familiar aims and skills. For centuries gold
from beyond the Sahara and the pepper substitute known as
grains of paradise had been available in the ports of North
Africa, drugs and spices from the East Indies in those of the
eastern Mediterranean. The desire to get to the source of these
supplies had led merchants to cross the Sahara and to travel

rely on advanced position-finding techniques. Using the familiar compass and estimating distance travelled by experience,
the feel of their ship and, while tacking, with the assistance of a
simple traverse board, pilots well into the sixteenth century
navigated by dead-reckoning. Accurate time-keeping is absolutely essential for determining longitude, only slightly less
crucial for fixing latitude, and the only time-piece sufficiently
practical for use at sea was the hourglass, never—on a pitch-
ing, swaying ship—a precise instrument even if an emergency
did not lead to its remaining unturned. There was an un-
bridgeable gap between an evolving shore-based theory and
what actually worked at sea. Mathematics, astronomy and precision instrument-making were not irrelevant to the process
of deliberate and sustained exploration but they determined
neither its timing nor its range.

These were determined by two things: a development in
geographical theory and a shift in the way in which men
imagined terrestrial space.

By 1480 geographers had devoted considerable attention to
the *Geographia* of Ptolemy and to the maps derived from his
text. The Ptolemaic world map showed the world as it had
been known to intelligent Romans of the second century; a
world that, thanks to Greek contact with India and guesses
derived from rumour and trade about what lay still further
east, gave a more or less accurate lay-out of Europe, the north
African coastline and Arabia, and allotted generous space to
the Indian Ocean—showing it, however, as an inland sea, its
southern shore washing the vast (and entirely speculative)
mass of Terra Incognita, which was shown north of and parallel to the Tropic of Capricorn, at which point it merged into
Africa. It showed that ships could sail clear from Africa to the
Indies (a term that telescoped the Malay peninsula, the East
Indies and China), but it also seemed to show that there was no
way of breaking into that route by sea; it gave a teasingly
clear view of the treasure and, at the same time, locked the
door on it. But Ptolemy was increasingly studied in conjunction with his predecessor, Strabo, who encouraged the idea
that Africa could in fact be circumnavigated, as did a third

ploration of the African coast had proceeded handhold by handhold; seamen approached the unknown, cape by cape and beach by beach, from the security of the known. Once the Cape had been rounded and contact made with Mozambique, they entered a highly sophisticated trading area with maps, pilots using quadrant and compass and a busy traffic of large ships. The Indian Ocean resembled an Arabic-speaking Mediterranean, and with interpreters from the Iberian peninsula or North Africa, Europeans could master its intricacies without too much difficulty though not, of course, without facing much danger and inevitable hardship. Once geographical theory and, consequently, maps had accepted the circumnavigability of Africa, contact with the far east was a matter of will and courage rather than of an imaginative conviction that justified an enormous leap across mere ocean.

That Cathay lay westwards across a great ocean had long been taken for granted. The implementation of this knowledge however, required not only suitable ships, adequate navigating techniques and men prepared to hazard their lives, but a way of imagining space expressed in cartographic terms as actually and invitingly open to exploration. And the shift from thinking of maps as records of what was known or surmised to seeing them as diagrams of the possible, as invitations to journeys that could be seen as an extension of ordinary voyages, was influenced more directly by art than by science or by travel itself. By the late fifteenth century an artist like Leonardo could not only record a landscape accurately as he stood before it, but imaginatively project his spatial thinking to the wider prospect of a bird's-eye view and, wider and higher still, to a detailed map of a whole province. Art helped the mind to think spatially by first training the eye. By helping men to 'see' the countryside as a whole, rather than as a mass of separate impressions, and training their imaginations by presenting them with imaginary but perfectly believable landscapes, the painter was enabling them to project the imagination beyond the frame of a painting, beyond what was visible to what could be conjectured, and similarly to urge it from the known part of the map to envis-

plan of operations. Certainly, in an age virtually without effective maps the bump of locality is likely to be well developed,
and the hunt sharpened an eye for terrain and the judging of
distance. If, however, there is an air of confusion and improvisation about the diplomatic and military events of the period it
is, at least in part, because men were literally unable to see
their goals.

The difficulty of collating written or verbal information
with a visualised spatial concept also accounts (though again,
only in part) for the general indifference of most Europeans to
the astounding enlargement of their geographical horizons.
The imagination simply could not follow the voyages, and accounts of what had been found were only attractive if they
were laced with the marvels and monsters of medieval travel
lore; the essential difference of the new lands and their peoples
could not be grasped because the imagination tugged them
back to Europe.

Narratives of voyages were printed from 1493, when an
account of Columbus' first voyage appeared in Rome, but
they did not acquire a significant readership until the middle
of the sixteenth century. Portentous as first the economic and
then the political consequences of trade and settlement overseas were to become, as yet, save to those directly involved
with overseas trade or the planning of voyages of discovery,
information about Africa, Asia and the Americas was irrelevant, and most humanist scholars were more concerned with
the re-discovery of the ancient world, which could be carried
on through words, the study of texts, than with paying attention to the discovery of the new, which involved a fresh
visualisation of space. Thoroughly typical was the reaction of
Marineo Siculo, who was teaching at Salamanca when Columbus was discussing geographical theory with his colleagues
there and who was one of Ferdinand of Aragon's official
historians. In all his voluminous writings there is only one
reference to the New World. He records the discovery of a
(presumed) Roman coin in Central America and smugly comments that 'this took the glory from our soldiers who were
boasting of their navigation, since the coin is proof that the

# CHAPTER II

# POLITICAL EUROPE

i

With hereditary, elective and joint monarchies, with broad-based and narrowly oligarchic republics, with independent and semi-independent confederations, with individual cities that operated as free agents and an emperor whose orders were virtually ignored by the vast majority of his subjects, the variety of ways in which government functioned is bewildering enough, even if we omit such anomalies as the papacy and the areas over which there was, to all intents and purposes, no government at all. * Yet in describing political events, whether they concern foreign policy and war, taxation and justice, struggles for power within a particular country, or the sense of relationship between a subject and his ultimate superior, the word government in this period has at least the merit of being less misleading than nation or state.

'Nation' then meant, as it had in the organisation of the General Councils of the church in the fifteenth century and still did in the social organisation of universities, a group of individuals with a common place of origin. It also conveyed a sense of the shared aims, experiences and sentiments which could be mobilised by government. It is, indeed, possible to speak of national feeling at this time and impossible to explain international affairs without stressing the strength of patriotism.† But the word nation in its modern usage calls up a more widely-felt sense of community than then existed and is inseparable from the notion of well-defined frontiers. Something like 'frontier thinking' was, indeed, involved when governments passed mercantilist economic legislation, or built fortresses to protect their territories, but being neither

* See Appendix. Europe c. 1500: a political gazetteer.
† See below, p. 104 seq.

by his election to the Empire in 1519, his inheritances in central Europe and the Netherlands and his marriage-trophy Spain as though they were one governmental unit.

In contrast to Asia, with its thinly spread populations and its gusts of supra-national religious enthusiasms, the European countries, especially in the west, were so squeezed together between the Atlantic, the North and Baltic Seas and the Mediterranean, their rivalries were so well defined, their con-quests at one another's expense so small, their administrative systems so effective, that it is tempting to see them as modern states. But even discounting the most 'Asiatic' regions of Europe, the extreme north where Lapps and Finns fished and followed their reindeer without needing to know who for the moment was ruling them, and the region between the Dniester and the Danube, a vaguely politicised zone of nomads, slavers and refugees, Europe, seen from within, was still far from being a system of thoroughly self-conscious and methodically administered political entities.

From the point of view of international relations, Europe can be considered as a closed world of its own. The Turks withdrew from their foothold on Italian soil at Otranto in 1481 and thereafter, apart from a sea war with Venice from 1499 to 1503, they were too occupied with fighting on their eastern border against Persia or with conquering Syria (1516) and Egypt (1517) to be of major concern to the European powers. Overseas, though by 1520 gigantic strides had been taken in the establishment of Spanish and Portuguese empires since Columbus' first voyage of 1492 and da Gama's landing at Calicut in 1498, the treaty of Tordesillas* had been effec-tive in persuading the seamen of the two countries to keep out of one another's way, and the era of interloping and rival settlements on the part of other countries still lay in the future. As far as international relations in Europe were con-cerned, the discoveries and the colonising movements which followed them had little more effect than to divert all of Portugal's and part of Castile's interest overseas. Aragon was

* See below p. 72.

stituted so rapidly. This was made possible by a transformation of diplomatic method. From the late fifteenth century the practice spread from Italy (where it was widely accepted) to the rest of western Europe of retaining diplomats *en poste* abroad for years at a time, so that the machinery for bringing about international agreements or changes of front was constantly in being. A second point is that the countries of Europe, especially those in the west, were to a hitherto unprecedented degree *able* to take a diplomatic initiative which could be followed up at once with cash and with armies.

Charles VIII was able to invade Italy with the largest army Europe had seen because his predecessor, Louis XI, had devoted a long reign (1461–83) to guiding France's economic recovery from the Hundred Years War. Ferdinand was enabled to intervene first on one side and then on the other because his joint reign with Isabella had restored order in the two kingdoms to such effect that the *reconquista* had been resumed, the Moorish kingdom of Granada conquered in 1492 and a well-trained army left idle. The end of the Wars of the Roses and the reign of Edward IV (1471–83) had restored peace and a re-tautening of government to England, a process that had been resumed under a Tudor monarch after the two year rule of Richard III (1483–5). Thus Charles VIII had to bribe Henry VII not to invade France in 1494 and Henry VIII was able to invade France in his successor's reign with little regard for the cost. In 1477 the Swiss had defeated (and killed) their chief enemy, Duke Charles the Bold of Burgundy, at Nancy. This left them secure enough to supply large numbers of their highly specialised pikemen to the early French campaigns in Italy. By 1499, after an even bloodier battle than Nancy, they had defeated an army sent against them by Maximilian and, freed from any practical dependence on the Empire, took part in the Italian wars increasingly as a polity and less as the supplier of troops to others. Only Germany itself remained as disunited as it had been in the middle of the fifteenth century and as lacking in effective central administration. Maximilian, as a result, was the weakest of the contestants who fought in the peninsula.

have bridged this continuity to some extent: these difficulties in the way of achieving some recognisable statehood were compounded by the fact that the destinies of these countries were determined by the self-interest of a particular class, the nobles, and by the family ties of rulers who formed a 'ring' which looked on the lands between Germany and Russia as common property to be shared out according to dynastic convenience rather than national interest. A similar uncertainty as to where effective authority lay slowed the move towards uniform administration and a higher degree of harmony between people and government in the Scandinavian countries. In Germany the particularist sentiment of certain towns and princes was so strong that they preferred to ally among themselves rather than invoke the protection of the imperial government. Thus the Swabian League was formed in the south in 1488 to contain the Swiss and prevent the expansion of Bavaria under its aggressive Wittelsbach duke. Within this mosaic of particularisms there were territories where government was at least as effective as it was, say, in England. One such territory was the Palatinate, but even here there were anomalies. Its ruler the elector had to accept that some of his powerful vassals should promise to support him not in his rôle as count palatine but in his personal guise as, say, the lord of Weinsberg. The Burgundian inheritance resembled Germany. From Franche-Comté to Brabant and Flanders all its components were subject to one ruler and his council, but they were too disparate in size, economic function and historical conditioning to function with real coherence. The industrialised regions were not only averse to being joined with the agricultural regions in the southern parts of the duchy but were intent on pursuing their own traditional rivalries, province against province, town against town. They had, moreover, strong personal loyalties of their own. The Guelderlanders, for instance, looked on the Egmont family as their natural leaders, not the Habsburgs. The Netherlands was not actually unworkable as a unit, but the process of achieving a measure of consent was immensely wasteful of time and money. Finally, within the Swiss Confederation there was no central power. Each canton remained

minister it as though it were a federation of independent powers. In Aragon, Ferdinand's will was particularly hampered by the need to defer to local customs in Catalonia, as was that of Isabella in the remotest part of her nation, Galicia, where she had to grope and sue for support among its rival chieftains. The Tudor writ, too, began to run haltingly as it neared the Scottish border, and even nearer the centre of government there were patches of territory, like the palatinate of Lancaster, the 'liberty' of Richmond and the soke of Peterborough, which retained traditional rights of self-determination in matters of law and, to a lesser extent, of taxation. Even Milan, a duchy brought forward in evidence by Jacob Burckhardt for his thesis that in Italy the state became a 'work of art', was so little a work of art that Lodovico Sforza, strongest of its rulers in this period, had to allow some of the leading families in the Milanese to issue their own statutes and to allow them to accept oaths of fealty from men in their neighbourhoods.

ii

If we take a republic, Florence, a monarchy with an undisputed succession of rulers, France, a joint monarchy, Spain, a monarchy with a new line of rulers, England, and the combination of independent federal and monarchical powers that was the Empire, narrative limits can be assigned to each of them which while by no means self-contained are something more than mere conveniences; they represent fairly well defined periods of political development and they roughly coincide. For Florence, such a period runs from 1478, the year of the Pazzi conspiracy to murder Lorenzo de' Medici and his brother, to the election in 1523 of the second Medici pope, Clement VII; for France from the resumption of royal control over Anjou and the duchy of Burgundy in 1481–2 to the Field of Cloth of Gold in 1520; for Spain from the Union of Castile and Aragon in 1479 to Charles of Habsburg's election as emperor in 1519; for England from Henry Tudor's accession in 1485 to the consolidation of Wolsey's control over foreign

was denounced even by his own party and he was forced to flee the city. The resentments that came to the surface represented many shades of opinion, but they expressed themselves in two major arguments: that Florence should be governed by a fairly small number of experienced men, subservient to no one family, and that political control should be far more widely spread than it had been at any time in the century. By now the Dominican prior of S. Marco, Girolamo Savonarola, had attained a remarkable ascendency over a large number of all classes in the city, based on a powerful pulpit manner in the evangelist tradition, a series of accurate prophecies, including Lorenzo's death and the coming of the French, and a down to earth concern with public issues. Almost certainly his support of the 'popular' argument enabled it to be put into effect. The constitution was redesigned with safeguards against the formation of parties and with a new feature that was as radical an inversion of the Medicean council of one hundred conceivable in the Europe of that time, a Great Council whose membership was open to one out of every four or five lay adult males living in the city.

The new form of government was at once put to the test of war, not through the direct participation of the citizens, but through heavy taxation for the hire of mercenaries, the psychological pressure of diplomatic isolation (for Florence stuck to the French alliance inaugurated by Piero), and actual threats to their territories from invading armies and from local crises such as Cesare Borgia's attempts to consolidate the fragmented political units of the neighbouring Romagna. Closest to Florentine hearts was the war that dragged on from 1495 to 1509 to regain Pisa; occupied by French troops as a guarantee that Florence would not cut Charles VIII's communications during his Neapolitan campaign of 1494–5, the city refused to return to Florentine domination when the French withdrew. And when that prolonged crisis was over another began, caused by Florence's resistance to the urging of Julius II to join the league he formed in 1511 to rally all Italy against the French. Continued opposition to that project led to the re-imposition of the Medici on the city by force of papal and Spanish troops

the government in the form in which Savonarola had known it.

For Florence the story that dates can tell is above all a constitutional one. For France it is predominantly one of wars.
From the death of Louis XI in 1483 one king followed another
without question or tumult, Charles VIII being succeeded by
Louis XII in 1498, Louis by Francis I in 1515. Louis XI's
policy of enforcing internal peace, keeping clear of major
foreign entanglements, encouraging trade and agriculture and
taking advice from men who shared his own taste for un-
glamorous hard work had succeeded well enough to allow a
country naturally rich in natural resources to recover from the
Hundred Years War. At the end of his reign two strokes of
luck nearly doubled the area of France directly belonging to
the crown. In 1481 the death of the last male representative of
the great feudal house of Anjou brought in the extensive
provinces of Anjou and Provence. In 1482 the Treaty of
Arras settled the problem of what was to become of Charles
the Bold's territories after his death in 1477 by giving Picardy
and the duchy of Burgundy to Louis. In marked contrast
to earlier periods, from 1482 to the conquests of Louis XIV
the history of France is that of very much the same geographical area—apart from Brittany. This duchy had tradi-
tionally conducted itself as an independent power. Again, a
fortunate death came to the aid of the crown. In 1488 duke
Francis II died, leaving the duchy to his daughter. Among her
numerous suitors Charles VIII proved most persuasive because
in 1491 he invaded Brittany with a large army and granted
terms only on condition that she marry him.

This recognisably modern 'France' continued to be governed on lines firmly sketched by Louis XI; the concentration
of authority within the king's council, definition of the competence of the other central organs of state, notably those dealing
with finance, and their relationship to that council, steady
erosion of local privileges in the interest of a uniform administration operating from Paris. This last policy proceeded slowly
enough to avoid any major confrontation between either
powerful individuals or corporations and the crown. The fact

Spanish troops expelled the French once more, and this time finally, in 1504.

By now military adventures in Italy had become something of a fashion. France's next attempt at conquest, through the League of Cambrai of 1508, was as part of an assault whereby France, Spain, Maximilian, Pope Julius II and the duke of Mantua were to partition the territories of Venice between them. The diplomatic preparations for Louis's part in this venture were necessarily elaborate. Louis was far more of a working monarch than Charles VIII, who could sign his own name only with difficulty, but though reasonably intelligent he was neither subtle nor patient and was fortunate in having a Wolsey in the shape of Georges, cardinal of Amboise, to take most of the burden of administration and negotiation from him. The allies' victory at Agnadello was complete but as in the case of Naples, occupation was followed by mutual jealousy. The allies, as we have seen, re-shuffled; Ferdinand and Julius and later Maximilian, joining forces against the French who by 1513 were forced not only out of the Veneto but out of the Milanese as well.

Flamboyant and cultivated, Francis I differed from his predecessors in every respect but militancy. Within a few months of his accession he was across the Alps and by the battle of Marignano convincingly won back Milan. The concordat of Bologna, in both which was conceded to Francis and which was withheld, reflected Leo X's grudging acceptance of the probability that France had come to Italy to stay.* So did the much-trumpeted Treaty of Cambrai of 1517 and its sister blue-print for lasting peace in Europe, the Treaty of London of the following year. On Maximilian's death in 1519 Francis even put himself forward as a candidate for the Empire. That glamorous if half-hearted bid, followed as it was next year by the portentous entertainment of the Field of Cloth of Gold, is chiefly notable because it represents an expenditure that, added to the costs of war in three reigns, could only come from a country so prosperous and—by the standards of the

* See below, p. 222.

grand masterships of the immensely wealthy military orders she made a remarkably bold stroke towards achieving this aim, too. She offered the first that fell vacant, that of Santiago, to Ferdinand, and he prudently refused. But this refusal meant that there was no serious opposition to his acceptance of the remaining two. Altogether, the affair of the grand masterships exemplified the successful union of talents as well as of crowns, with Ferdinand's astuteness balancing his wife's approach, a blend of impulsive pragmatism and—especially in religious matters—idealism.

The union itself was quickly followed by another measure designed to produce cash and cut down the power of the nobles *vis à vis* the crown: the Act of Resumption of 1480, whereby they were required to hand back all crown lands they had occupied during the disturbances since 1464. In the same year the royal council of Castile was reformed on lines that seriously maimed the initiative of the great feudatories. And in 1482 Isabella diverted their energies and gave her new administration time to stabilise by re-opening the centuries-long crusade against the Moors, now concentrated in the Muslim kingdom of Granada.

For ten years the history of Spain was largely one of war in the south and consolidation at the centre, and if there is any recognisable break in the period we are treating it comes in 1492. In that year Granada finally fell and was incorporated in Castile. Six months later Christopher Columbus at last got the backing he had been demanding for years and set off to make the first recorded European contact with the West Indies. In one sense this voyage, and those that followed it represented a transference of the mood of *reconquista* overseas. But just as the war against Granada had combined the service both of God and of internal order, the transatlantic voyages were designed to produce both Christians and gold. More purely idealistic, or at least more singlemindedly doctrinaire, was the third chief event of that year, the forcible expulsion of all professing Jews.*

The bull *Inter caetera* whereby Spain obtained exclusive rights over her New World discoveries from the Spanish pope

* See below, p. 193 seq.

crusade against the Moors across to the north African coast, where Oran was captured in 1509, and he obtained from Julius II the right to appoint to all ecclesiastical benefices in the New World, a right he and Isabella had already obtained for Granada.

This was the first of the policies of the Catholic Kings (the title Ferdinand and Isabella had been granted in 1494 for their services to the church) which Charles followed after Ferdinand's death in 1516. His advisers persuaded the pope to grant the crown the right to appoint to bishoprics throughout Spain, thus obtaining the most tractable of all the national branches of the Catholic church in Europe. It was some years before he picked up the other threads of his predecessor's policies. Arriving in Spain in 1517, unable to speak Spanish and surrounded by Flemings, his personal unpopularity brought a resentful halt to political changes of moment until he learned to govern Spain as a Spaniard in the years after his election to the Empire in 1519.

As with Spain, the first responsibility of government in England was the imposition of law and order and the re-establishment of effective royal power. In England the task was eased because the means of exerting the crown's authority were already established by long precedent and incorporated in financial, judicial and consultative institutions, which, given favourable circumstances and sound leadership, could produce strong and orderly rule. In Castile and to a lesser extent in Aragon, the sovereigns had to invent; in England their chief task was to restore.

Some progress was made in this direction during the 1470s by Edward IV, not so much in checking the slide towards the sort of unplanned decentralisation that resulted from the retaining of private armies and from the feuds that persisted between the supporters of York and Lancaster, but in putting the central organs of government back to work in the interest of the country rather than of a clique. Edward died in 1483. The succession of his twelve year old son Edward V provoked the closet-skirmish that was the prelude to the last of the Wars of the Roses: a struggle for control of the government be-

opposition remained. Around Lambert Simnel, posing as the imprisoned earl of Warwick, rallied enough disaffection for Henry to have to lance it with a battle, the rout at Stoke in 1487 which left Simnel a prisoner in his hands. A graver threat, and a much more long-lasting one, was Perkin Warbeck, posing as Edward V's brother the duke of York. That Henry's problems were not ones merely of domestic order was shown by the support Warbeck obtained first in France, then in the Netherlands and successively in the Empire, Ireland and Scotland before he found himself let down by the men of Cornwall, whose traditional resistance to central authority he had relied on to give him an army. His career as an imposter had lasted for six years before he surrendered in 1497. Two years later Henry was still concerned enough about plots against the regime to have both Warbeck and the still imprisoned earl of Warwick executed.

Yet by this time Henry had already taken steps to protect himself through a ring of foreign alliances. By the treaty of Medina del Campo in 1489 his two-year-old son Arthur was contracted to marry Ferdinand's daughter Catherine. The treaty of Étaples with France in 1492 put an end to the support Henry had been giving to Brittany's struggle for independence; support given partly in his role as claimant to the throne of France and partly because friendship with Brittany was the surest way of keeping down piracy in the Channel. By 1496 a peace settlement with the Netherlands reduced the danger of support for a rival coming from that source, in spite of continuing economic rivalry. Nearer home, Ireland was punished for having supported Warbeck by laws ('Poynings laws') passed at Drogheda in 1494 which theoretically made Ireland completely subservient to the English crown, and in 1502 a marriage was arranged between princess Margaret and James IV of Scotland. Internally the reign was less a matter of events than of processes. Financially the crown was given a greatly enhanced freedom of action by an act of resumption in 1481 which paralleled Isabella's of 1480, but apart from that Henry played the role of the good steward rather than of the constitutional innovator or the dashing pro-

disparity between geography and constitution. The emperor spoke as the political leader of Germany but the Germans did not back him up. This was only to a small degree because of the elective, rather than hereditary nature of the imperial title. To all intents and purposes the Empire was hereditary in the Habsburg family; Maximilian succeeded his father Frederick III in 1493 and was succeeded in turn by his grandson Charles in 1519. The chief reason was the lack of an imperial machinery to connect the policies of the emperors with the pockets of the multitudes of princes, knights, and cities who treated their constitutional place within the Empire as peripheral to their own interests. This constitutional place was not ignored. Indeed, it was acknowledged that certain problems, brigandage, private war and, in the south west, population pressure, could not be dealt with on the local level. Both the components of the Empire and the emperor himself wanted parts of the machinery to work, but their efforts were hamstrung by a failure to agree on how it should work. And this failure, and hence the failure of the emperor to receive backing outside his own hereditary lands, was thrown into relief by the consequences of the Burgundian Duke Charles the Bold's death at the battle of Nancy in 1477.

Thanks to his marriage to Charles' daughter Mary, Maximilian received the lion's share of the duke of Burgundy's lands. He had to fight France for them but by the Peace of Senlis in 1493 he retained Franche-Comté, Luxembourg and the wealthily industrialised Netherlands, governed on his behalf by his son Philip from 1494 and then, on Philip's death in 1506, by the young Charles, chiefly under the influence of his aunt Margaret. It was this acquisition of land in the west that brought the issue of reform of the imperial constitution into urgent relief. Emperors habitually put the interest of their own territories before those of Germany as a whole. Now, to the political interests of the old Habsburg lands— hostility to Venice, defence against the Turks, fishing in the dynastic waters of Bohemia and Hungary—was added the challenge of having an unfriendly France as a neighbour. And this came at a time when France, plunging repeatedly into

authority. In 1500 he had to accept the *Reichsregiment*, a supreme governing body of which he was president but which could legislate for the Empire without him. His military plans again petered out, but at least he had the satisfaction of seeing the new council wither away as an effective organ of state within a couple of years. It was the last serious attempt at reform before Maximilian's death.

But if subsequent diets were slightly less critical, the emperor continued to cut a poor figure abroad. In 1496 he had vainly attacked the Tuscan port of Livorno as Lodovico Sforza's ally against Florence. In 1509 his only contribution to the war against Venice was the unsuccessful siege of Padua. In 1516 he invaded the Milanese but ran out of money after he had been in Milan for a single day; his troops deserted and he returned to Austria in humiliation.

From 1493 to 1519 the history of the Empire is only marginally the history of Germany. That is above all the history of the individual principates, the self-governing ecclesiastical territories and the great cities which made up the German-speaking world. Maximilian tried to give them a common destiny through fervent propaganda on behalf of a revived imperial leadership. And he failed. His success lay in the government of his own lands and in a dynastic policy that made his successor the ruler of more than half of western Europe.

iii

Except for a few instances, the chief domestic aim of government, in these five states as elsewhere, was not to innovate but to restore. However, as Guicciardini pointed out in his comments on Machiavelli's *Discourses*, any attempt to reproduce something that has happened in the past necessarily produces something novel because of intervening circumstances. What gives the governments of this period some air of novelty was the number of precedents they exhumed or refurbished and the speed with which they did it, the fairly general acqui-

*stag*, in Castile and Aragon the *cortes*, in France and the Netherlands meetings of estates, in England parliament. All these bodies had been shaped primarily by the crown's need for special taxes for military purposes and for the public support that was necessary if they were to be collected. They were susceptible to manipulation by the crown, particularly if the nobility were on its side, but the principle of redress of grievances in return for grants of cash was common to all of them, and rulers were naturally loath to summon them except in case of great need. Before the costs of her and Ferdinand's wars in Italy mounted seriously, Isabella let fourteen years elapse without calling the Castilian *cortes* together; Henry VII only called one parliament between 1497 and his death in 1509. The period was in general a testing time rather than a turning point in the development of national assemblies. At its close the decline of the French estates general was not yet confirmed; at the other extreme, the regular partnership of crown and parliament, later to be characteristic of English government, was hardly anticipated.

A more important development was the increasing number of professionals employed in government, for they provided continuity, a concept of service detached from blood or possession, a sense of impersonal, pervasive and accreting activity on behalf of government rather than of a particular ruler. From royal councils to local administration the number of men employed for their skill alone increased. From Russia to the Palatinate and Spain and England the secretary became a key member of the administration. It is no accident that the Empire, where the civil service was weakest, failed to produce either an effective imperial or federal administration—yet even there the spirit of the more impersonal state-to-be was expressed by one of Maximilian's learned councillors who complained that nothing ever got done because the emperor himself was constantly meddling.

This move towards an impersonal element in government in no way diminished the personal rôle of the ruler or the image he presented to his people. Every subject, said Charles VIII's chancellor when introducing him to the estates general

to the local estates, invited the towns to endorse his pre-invasion treaties of 1493 and justified the invasion itself to them. Monarchs still extracted personal oaths of allegiance from individuals and towns, thus indicating that the crucial loyalties were expected to be felt for the sovereign rather than for the state. Henry's visit to Worcester was part of a programme followed by all rulers to show themselves to the people. Erasmus warned the future Charles V that 'nothing so alienates the affections of his people as for [the ruler] to take pleasure in living abroad, for then they seem to be neglected by him to whom they wish to be most important.' In illness and old age, Louis XI, terrified of assassination, shut himself up at Plessis-les-Tours, strengthening it with spikes and iron pill-boxes from which archers could shoot at anyone trying to gain an entrance. He dismissed most of his attendants for fear that they should poison him. Yet in order to make it clear that though in seclusion he had not ceased to rule, he increased his diplomatic activity and invented excuses to correspond with countries with which diplomatic negotiations could not credibly be carried on. According to Commines he sent to Spain for mastiffs, Valencia for 'little shaggy dogs', to Sicily for a mule, to Naples for horses, even to Sweden and Denmark for elk and reindeer.

So far were they from trusting to administrative forms and centralising policies to preserve loyalty to the man as well as obedience to the machine that rulers up-graded their titles. The grand duke Ivan III of Russia had himself styled 'sovereign of all Russia', his successor, Vasili, referred to himself as tsar, or emperor. From the neutral and objective 'king' Henry VII had become by 1504 'our most dread sovereign lord'. The titles given in proclamations emphasised the wars were between rulers, not between states. In 1485, when England and France were on friendly terms, the French king was referred to as Henry's 'most dearest cousin, Charles of France'. Five years later, France was an enemy, its ruler simply 'Charles the French king.' In 1492 alliance brought Henry to refer to 'the right high and mighty prince his cousin of France'. War in 1513 led to a return to the formula 'Louis the French king',

various. Proclamations and manifestos were distributed for
reading from the pulpit. Yea-saying men of letters were employed to trumpet their employers' fame and the rightness
of their causes. The fine arts were pressed into service even
when the audiences they impressed were necessarily small.
Threatened by proposals to call a general council of the
church, Sixtus IV commissioned Botticelli to warn the con-
ciliarists of the fate that befell rebels to God's appointed by
means of his fresco The Punishment of Corah. Julius II, conscious that heretics who attacked the doctrine of transubstantiation were also attacking the priests who alone could produce the miracle, had Raphael paint the Miracle of Bolsena,
with its wafer stained with blood.* Medals were struck with
political slogans. Even everyday coins could carry a political
message. After Isabella's death Ferdinand, though legally no
more than regent in Castile, had coins minted with the in-
scription 'Ferdinand and Joanna, King and Queen of Castile,
Leon and Aragon'. Nor was the drama neglected. Sanna-
zaro's *The triumph of fame* celebrated Ferdinand's conquest of
Granada for the benefit of his cousin Ferrante of Naples. Konrad Celtis wrote a play which commemorated Maximilian's
defeat of the Bohemian army in 1504 and coupled with it an
exhortation to the emperor to take a crusading army to Constantinople—a project for which Maximilian had long sought
money and troops. Whether the poet and dramatist Pierre
Gringore was actually sponsored by Louis XII is not clear, but
his writings certainly followed the king's policies very closely:
anti-Venetian in 1509, when France was about to attack
Venice, anti-papal in 1512, when Louis was trying to bully
Julius II with the help of a general council of the church.

The use of popular phrases in Gringore's propaganda plays
suggests that they were written for audiences with a mixed
social background. Still wider audiences were reached by the

---

* To memorialise Sweden's release from the coils of Denmark
Sven Sture commissioned Bernt Notke to make the equestrian statue
of St. George and the dragon—an action paralleled by the erection
of Donatello's Judith and Holofernes in front of Florence's civic
palace to symbolise the expulsion of the Medici.

which was then extended still further by published descriptions.

The effect of realism in the fine and graphic arts and in
portraits on medals and coins, of the press and of the newly
elaborate pageant and the masque-play was to make the image
of the ruler so vivid that for the majority of men exposed to
these media it helped to obscure the growth of bureaucratic
institutions and the increasing grip of government on the
nation as a whole. Printed collections of statutes, proclamations and legal decisions helped to give a circle of educated
men, for the most part lawyers, a clearer view of government
as a substantive, evolving whole, though as the volume of
original law-making was still small and the citation of centuries-old statutes frequent, the potential power of government to interfere progressively and minutely with men's lives
was difficult to grasp. And this was particularly true at a time
when diplomacy, wars and highly publicised dynastic marriages were continually drawing attention to the personal rôle
of the prince or his *alter ego*, a Wolsey in England, an Amboise
in France—in decisions affecting the destinies of peoples.*

iv

Before describing Utopia, Thomas More's imaginary traveller,
Raphael Hythlodaeus, was asked why he did not put the
wisdom he had accumulated overseas at the disposal of some
ruler in Europe. His answer was that 'many have done it in
published books' but vainly, because princes do not want to be
told to rule uprightly. 'Come now,' he continued, 'suppose I
were at the court of the French King and sitting in his privy
council. In a most secret meeting, a circle of his most astute
councillors over which he personally presides is setting its
wits to work to consider by what crafty mechanisms he may
keep his hold on Milan and bring back into his power the
Naples which has been eluding his grasp; then overwhelm
Venice and subjugate the whole of Italy; next bring under
his sway Flanders, Brabant and, finally, the whole of Bur-

† See further on this topic, below, p. 104 seq.

What reception from my listeners, my dear More, do you
think this speech of mine would find?'*

More's reply, of course, was 'not a very favourable one'.
His own revulsion from war-mongering was such that he made
the Utopians prefer assassination, supporting rival factions,
bringing an enemy's rivals on his back: anything in fact, that
intelligence could invent rather than having recourse to the
humiliatingly animal-like phenomenon of combat.

His portrait of the council meeting was only mildly a caricature and was based on the actual policies of France at the
beginning of Francis I's reign. Looking back from 1516, indeed, a man of peaceable mood born, as More was, in 1478,
could hardly fail to reflect on the number of wars that had
taken place in his life-time and the scant changes in prosperity, frontier or regime to which they had led in Europe.
It was only in the east that war had led to dramatic and lasting changes. Turkish expansion into Europe had already overwhelmed Serbia and Bosnia and reached the Adriatic. The
occupation of Otranto and the even more daring raid that took
Turkish cavalry round Venice into the neighbourhood of
Vicenza in 1499, were mere demonstrations, though shock-
ing ones; the reluctance of Turkish troops to winter away
from their homes put a geographical limit to their actual con-
quests. But in 1516 and 1517, in two superbly energetic campaigns, Selim I conquered Syria and Egypt with long-term
consequences to Mediterranean trade greater than any produced by a purely European conflict. In Russia, too, armies
built Ivan III's control outwards from Moscow and supported
his successor Vasili's completion of the control of Ryazan
and the coup which abolished the independence of Pskov.
Armies cut the threads held in Hungary during the reign of
Matthias Corvinus, and from his death in 1490 Silesia, Moravia, Moldavia and Wallachia swung away into other orbits;
Polish, Lithuanian or Turkish.

* Tr. G. C. Richards in *The Complete Works of St. Thomas
More*, Vol. 4, ed. Edward Surtz and J. H. Hexter (Yale U.P. 1965)
87–91. Myron P. Gilmore drew attention to the illustrative value
of this passage in *The World of Humanism* (N.Y., 1952) 155.

This Utopian project foundered with the imperial election of the following year and wars in Italy—for Francis could not expect to conquer Charles' heartlands themselves—started up on a larger scale than ever. Even within Italy itself, while there were many changes of régime as the states paid off old scores among themselves, changed their own governments, sought foreign protection or found themselves temporarily occupied, there were only minor adjustments of borders. Nor were the campaigns outside Italy which were fought as by-products of the chief struggle notably successful. Ferdinand did not conquer the whole of Navarre. Henry sold Tournai back to France five years after taking it. Writing when the fate of Milan and Naples was still in doubt, it was natural for More to suggest that the gains of war did not justify the sacrifices made for them. Indeed, apart from the Spanish conquests in northern and southern Italy the lasting changes in political control in this period were not the result of war. Venice obtained Cyprus from its ruler Catarina Cornaro in 1488 as the result of a cash bargain, albeit backed by the threat of force. The kings of France were indebted for the extension of their power not so much to arms as to confiscation for treason (the Armagnac and Alençon territories), failure of heirs (Anjou, Maine, Provence) and marriage (Brittany). The greatest accumulation of power of all was brought into the hands of Charles V by election and inheritance. Why, then, was there so much war-mongering?

Almost everybody in Europe took wars for granted. In Bohemia a few descendants of the Hussites believed that Christ had come to deliver the world from war, that Christians should verily turn the other cheek and meet violence with non-resistance. More and Erasmus were among the very few who put forward pacifist ideas on humanitarian grounds. The church's doctrine of the Just War—that it was legitimate to fight on the authority of a legally constituted superior, for a just cause and with righteous intent—was not in itself ignoble, but, as Erasmus pointed out, 'among such great and changing vicissitudes of human events, among so many treaties and agreements which are now entered into, now rescinded, who

men still lingered in judicial thought, and war was but an extension of this notion. In a primarily agrarian world the bulk of litigation was about land. Land was avidly grasped however far away from the chief estate, however unproductive or difficult to administer. As the greatest landlords in their countries, rulers applied the same standards to territories as distant as was Naples from Paris, and warfare in these circumstances was but litigation pursued by other means.

The lack of a clear idea of natural or linguistic frontiers is crucial to an understanding of this state of mind. So is the equation: power equals land. Land for the subject still carried with it an aura of private justice and personal homage even though governments were doing their best to dissipate it. Outside the burgher republics, social standing was above all a matter of acres, forests, tenants, petitioners in the forecourt, retainers at the common table, muniments spelling out privileges—even if they no longer obtained. For the ruler as inheritor or conqueror, land had a value for its own sake. To chide the kings of France for striking south to Naples, which produced little more than grain (a commodity which France seldom had to import) and could only be reached by immensely vulnerable lines of communication, is reasonable but unrealistic. Henry VIII has been scolded* for seizing territories in France which were bound to be impermanent. Why did he not spend the money on making Calais, already English and commercially valuable, really strong instead? To conquer France itself, to assert his fragile claim to its throne: these things were impossible. Yet Henry's coinage continued to style him king of France. So strong was the urge to acquire land that it lingered symbolically long after the actuality was dead. Catarina Cornaro, dwindled to proprietress of the tiny town of Asolo, styled herself Queen of Cyprus still, and Queen, too, of Jerusalem and Armenia.

Maximilian's plan to obtain Brittany in 1490 by a secret marriage to its duchess at a time when he was in scant control of his own south German inheritance, was, given the temper

* Recently, very severely indeed in *Army Royal* by C. G. Cruikshank (Oxford 1969).

cause the chain reactions that followed from war were not checked by any clear concept of neutrality. A country could try to stay out of trouble, but old allegiances would be invoked, rights of passage called for; more persuasive than the plea 'I want to be left alone' was the counter-argument 'My cause is just, therefore as a Christian government you should support it.'

Economic motivation played but a small part in a decision to go to war. Piracy, endemic in the Baltic, the English Channel and the Mediterranean, was dealt with by reprisal, licensed counter-piracy and confiscations on the part of individuals, rather than by war. Over the centuries, market agreements between neighbour nations, the establishment of staple towns, international fairs and trading companies—an accumulation of devices had been worked out which enabled imports and exports, raw materials or finished goods to flow in reasonable accord with the economic needs of individual countries. Rulers were more easily moved by the past than by a vision of future balance sheets, Ivan by the desire to recover 'all the Russian land of old', Maximilian to reassert the centuries-old claims of the Empire in north Italy, Charles VIII and Louis XII to reactivate their own families' claims in the peninsula. Though the opportunities occurred in the present, the justifications for war were to be found in history, a litter of claims that could be resurrected with a fine show of legality and could commonly be associated with the grievances of exiles or malcontents: Louis XII's claim to Milan went back to a marriage of 1389 and his first invading army was led by a Milanese, Gian Giacomo Trivulzio, who had been banished by Lodovico Sforza.

The medieval doctrine of the Just War assumed that the decision to open hostilities was a personal, not a collective decision. The position had not changed during the intervening centuries. 'The common folk do not go to war of their own accord,' wrote More, 'but are driven to it by the madness of kings.' And Erasmus similarly laid the blame for 'that madness of war that has persisted so long and disgracefully among Christians' at the door of the European princes. The personal

men already trained in the use of their weapons. But such an army was no longer an effective fighting force. The noble cavalryman was a dwindling asset in the face of pike and gun. The local levies were seldom properly trained, their arms and equipment were frequently inadequate or missing and were in any case old-fashioned: sword, bill and bow at a time when pike (which required regular group training) and hand gun or arquebus (expensive and distrusted in lower class hands in peacetime) were becoming the key infantry weapons. When to this is added the reluctance of townsmen to leave their occupations and peasants their harvests for the uncertainties of a campaign, it is apparent that the old system had to some extent broken down; those who planned wars had to take into account the engagement and pay of mercenaries. The extent of discussion about the rival merits of native *versus* mercenary troops, *ad hoc versus* permanent armies, points to the same conclusion.

This debate was least urgent in Castile, whose mainly pastoral economy led to underemployment and made recruiting easy, and in Switzerland, another pastoral country and one, moreover, accustomed to defending its independence by arms. It was liveliest in Italy, particularly in the republics, where unbellicose burghers had long relied on hired professionals to do their fighting and were perturbed by the difficulty of controlling them, but the issues were also of concern to France and England. Mercenaries were trained men who brought their own equipment. But they were expensive and had to be paid promptly, their commanders did not always see eye to eye with the native leadership, discipline was more difficult to keep in multi-national armies, orders more difficult to pass. National resentment could cause trouble when mercenaries were used for garrison duty. A permanent national army avoided delay in starting a campaign, meant that trained men were always at the ready, cut down the need to enter into alliances simply in order to obtain extra troops, enabled the lessons of one war to be incorporated in the methods used in the next. On the other hand it was expensive to maintain a military establishment in peacetime, and a standing army might

required and the difficulty of hiring carts and draft animals when passing through country where the farming season was in full swing. Frequently there was not enough coin to pay the troops, though experience had shown that this was bad for morale in the case of native troops and disastrous in the case of mercenaries, who could desert *en masse* or even turn on their employers. But this very unrealism made it easier for war to be declared when a king and his entourage decided on it. And it was reflected in the reliance placed on allies.

The freedom of England from civil wars, the consolidation of French territory coupled with a striking economic recovery from the Hundred Years War, the union of the Spanish crowns and the end of the crusade against the Moors, the succession of the would-be warlike Maximilian on the death of the more cautious Frederick III : these developments produced an atmosphere in international relations in the late fifteenth century all the more tense because of the common interest in Italy and in the bargains that could be struck among the powers competing there. Both the tempo and the temper of diplomacy were affected. Though the resident diplomat was usually of a social rank too low to sign a treaty, he could urge negotiations to a point at which a more formal embassy could endorse it. On the other hand, though it was easier to induce in these agents a sense that their business was to serve the interests of their home governments and not to make up their own minds nor apply their own moral scruples to political matters, they found it more difficult to get information or be treated with real confidence than did the traditional noble or episcopal ambassador. Nor did their home governments always treat the information sent back in despatches with the confidence due to them. And information continued to be sought by other means, through spies and tapping the mercantile news networks. There is little doubt that the presence of rival diplomats at courts, the bribes and other underhand methods they were at times forced to use, added an air of distrust to the diplomacy they helped to speed up.

Though there were a few lasting themes—English use of Flanders to counter French intrigues with Scotland; Spain's

# CHAPTER III

# INDIVIDUAL AND COMMUNITY

i

This was not an age in which the individual had grown away from the need to be linked with others. Indeed, it is probably true that from the points of view of emotion, self-interest and intellect these links were stronger than ever: the family a more self-conscious unit, the gild a more stalwart protector, the town a source of greater pride, membership of a nation somewhat more meaningful, the international fellowship of scholarship certainly more warming. Only the always vague notion of belonging to the super-community of Christendom was on the wane.

Christendom as a notion was a commonplace, but in the main it was kept alive by two elements well removed from practical politics: nostalgia for the days of the crusader, nourished by chivalrous literature, and the individual's hope that he could cancel out his sins by contributing to the recapture of the holy places—a motive considerably weakened by the efficient tourist service run by the Mamluk rulers of the bible lands.

Most popes, indeed, took their crusading duties seriously. In 1481 Sixtus IV, with immense effort, raised a fleet and an army to dislodge the Turks from Otranto. He had hoped to persuade this force to cross the Adriatic and recapture the Dalmatian fortress town of Valona, but their immediate task accomplished, the ships and troops slipped away to their homes. In 1484 Innocent VIII called on all the rulers of Europe to send ambassadors to Rome to plan a crusade. His legates were still trying to rouse the powers to interest in 1488. In 1500 Alexander VI issued a similar summons, which was similarly ignored. In 1517 Leo X worked out a scheme which even went so far as planning how the conquered territories of the

the sultan Bayezid assured his viziers that nothing would
come of European projects for a crusade. 'The Christians,' he
pointed out, 'fight constantly among themselves ... One says
to another, "Brother, help thou me to-day against this prince,
and tomorrow I will help thee against that one." Fear not, there
is no concord amongst them. Everyone takes care of himself
only; no one thinks of the common interest.' In 1516 Erasmus
confirmed this observation in *The Education of a Christian
Prince*, written for the future Charles V: 'Every Angle hates
the Gaul, and every Gaul the Angle, for no other reason than
that he is an Angle. The Irishman, just because he is an Irishman, hates the Briton; the Italian hates the German; the
Swabian, the Swiss; and so on throughout the list. District
hates district and city hates city.' And indeed, when the
Venetian ambassador asked Henry VIII in 1516 for aid against
the common foe of Christendom he got the following answer
'you are wise, and in your prudence will understand that no
general expedition against the Turks will ever be effected so
long as such treachery prevails among the Christian powers
that their sole thought is to destroy one another.' Ivan III,
theoretically well placed to organise a flank attack, preferred
negotiation to crusade. Florence took advantage of the fact
that Bayezid, who succeeded Mohammed the Conqueror in
1481, was more eager to consolidate than to extend his power,
to increase its trading colony in Constantinople.

As for the Iberian peninsula, since the beginning of Portuguese exploration down the west coast of Africa there had
been a more profitable and, for the western powers, politically
more purposeful outlet for the crusading impulse. When the
Portuguese passed on from the gold of Guinea to the spices of
Calicut, King Manuel explained in a letter of 1499 to Ferdinand and Isabella that 'the principal motive of this enterprise
has been, as with our predecessors, the service of God our
lord and our own advantage.' And Columbus, well aware that
the Catholic monarchs wanted a cash return from his voyage,
knew too that they would be glad to hear that conditions in
the West Indies were 'propitious for the realisation of what I
conceive to be the principal wish of our most serene king,

might shift attention from the personal responsibility of the ruler.

Similarly with justice. There was a steady advance of royal at the expense of local or personal justice, but whether this was administered by a familiar face, like that of the English justice of the peace, or a royal judge on circuit or by one of the central appeal courts, the image was not of an impersonal law but of a king acting out the most traditional of his roles, composing the differences of his subjects. The higher the plaintiff fought his way through the courts, the nearer he came not to the majesty of the law but to the majesty of the king. And in recognition of this role rulers continued to accept individual petitions for the redress of a grievance either, as through the English parliament, at one remove, or, as was Ferdinand and Isabella's practice, in person on a day set aside for this purpose. And they continued to make liberal use of their prerogative of pardon.

The third expectation, that rulers should live off the income from their personal possessions as much as possible and impose the minimum tax that would make the running of a war possible, was increasingly disappointed. Burgeoning administrations, larger, more specialised and thus more highly paid armies: the costs of government were rising and had to be passed on. Not everyone was threatened by banditry, not everyone went to law, but customs dues and sales taxes—especially on essentials like salt—made taxation a matter of almost universal concern. But, again, the common reaction to unpopular taxes was not to sense an inexorable extension of central control but either to bargain for a straight *quid pro quo* in the form of redress of grievances or the grant of privileges, or to complain that the king was ill advised, the victim of corrupt ministers and greedy courtiers.

Though agents of central government were inserted into local administration this was most clearly seen to be happening by the very small minority of Europeans who lived in towns. A linked development, the decreasing use of national representative bodies, meant that government, in the sense of the ruler's chief officers and their staffs, were actually negotiated

the country or, among southerners, from an assembly which would require them all, from Toulouse to Provence, to dilute their regional identities. An Italian coming home from a sojourn in the north might long to be back in 'Italy', but once home his horizon shrank to a desire to be in his own native land, Florence or Rimini or Naples. It is understandable that in Bohemia, where many of the merchants, prelates and landlords were German, it was difficult for the lower reaches of society to look towards government with any sense of identification with it. But in most parts of Europe 'state' law had a tough struggle to supplant local law, which however imperfect, was thought to be more 'natural' than the justice administered by the highly trained appeal judges of the capital. There was widespread anger in Germany over the inclination of princes to employ judges and chancery officials trained in Roman law. This was a capital mistake, said a Bavarian knight in 1499, 'for these men of the law do not know our habits, and when they do, they are not prepared to accept our customs.' Expressing the same anti-centralising vein was a protest from the estates of Württemberg in 1514; the duke should only employ men who will 'judge according to the ancient customs and usages and not trouble his poor subjects.'

By the time Francis I came to the throne in 1515 France was the supreme example in Europe of what a deliberately centralising policy could achieve. What it could not achieve, there or elsewhere, was an extension of the range of the individual's loyalties, a broadening of the circle of causes for which he was prepared to make sacrifices. The great magnate might become a provincial governor, acting for the crown, but the loyalty and awe with which he was regarded was not thereby channelled to the capital. In every town, even in some large villages, one or two of the leading inhabitants were employed as royal officials, usually in conjunction with their normal occupation of merchant or lawyer. They were linked by couriers and itinerant administrators to the judicial and financial courts in Paris. But these officials were still regarded as local men, and they had a continual struggle to impose royal decrees on local habits. An extract from the journal-chronicle of Benoît Mail-

to defer to local sentiment and to woo co-operation by invoking the glamour of the royal name. No reverberation emanated
from 'the government'; appointments, proclamations, edicts
had to come from the king.

The king's name was familiar in every court where royal
justice was administered. At Nottingham sessions, Henry
Gorrall was presented because it was said that he 'on the 26th
day of September in the 13th year of the reign of King Henry
the Seventh (1497) with force and arms, to wit, with a club
and knife, threw out a dead and putrid horse into the streets
of our Lord the King at Nottingham aforesaid, to the grievous
nuisance of the lieges of our said Lord the King, and against
his peace.' There was keen public interest in royal births,
marriages and deaths. Pamphlets recorded the ceremonial
visits of monarchs to cities in their realms and woodcuts
commemorated their coronations. This constant citing of the
monarch's name, this feeling for royalty did little, however, to
link men into a nation-wide community of subjects. In 1495,
during an attempt to settle a demarcation dispute between
Languedoc and Provence, a commissioner from Provence
(which had been annexed to the crown in 1481) was sent to set
up the provincial arms on the Îles du Rhône. In so doing he
came across a post to which the royal arms had been fixed. His
reaction was revealing. He removed his hat and knelt before
this symbol of royal power, then stood up, removed it and left
it in the sacristy of a local church 'where relics are conserved'.

Inheritance, dynastic marriages, the fortunes of war: it was
taken for granted that the limits of a country's jurisdiction
might fluctuate; the image of 'France' was still further weakened by the accompanying notion, 'the lands ruled for the
time being by the French king'. Moreover, when French royal
power made a step forward it did so to a modern end but by
medieval means, by invoking inheritance or feudal law, or by
answering an appeal for aid or protection; each new link with
a district or town was thus seen in isolation from any centralising policy as a whole and in terms of the feudal contract,
theoretically revocable and based on the mutual performance
of obligations. The machinery of the nation state of the future

is was the Gauls who conquered Germany [Charlemagne] protected the papacy [Pepin and Charlemagne] and freed the Holy Land [the crusades].' Rome had brought cruelty and subjugation in her wake, Christophe de Langueil pointed out in 1510, but the Gauls had always acted with justice and virtue. 'In arts and sciences', moreover, 'France is superior to Italy: she has produced from her own soil more men eminent in all ways than all other nations put together.' No wonder that the humanist lawyer Guillaume Budé was moved to dedicate one of his treatises, the *De Asse* of 1515, which dealt with Roman coinage, simply 'to the Genius of France'. No wonder, on the other hand, that the Alsatian Jakob Wimpfeling denied that the descendants of the Nervii had ever conquered the descendants of Arminius. The French claimed that the good German land between the Vosges and the Rhine belonged to them. 'Where are there any traces of the French language?' he asked, 'there are no books in French, no monuments, no letters, no epitaphs, no deeds or documents.' As for the Italians, what need was there to defer to them? They had been sunk in ignorance while the tenth century German nun Hroswitha was writing the plays which Celtis had re-discovered and dedicated to the Elector Frederick. Instead, the Germans should assert the European leadership that was theirs by character, culture and history. 'Truly', wrote von Hutten in his dialogue *Trias Romana*, 'it is a great and excellent deed to bring it about by persuading, exhorting, driving and impelling that the fatherland come to recognise its own debasement and arm itself to win back its ancient liberty.'

This jingoism of the intelligentsia evoked little public response. Pope Julius II could remind all Italians of their common inheritance from ancient Rome when calling on them to back his determination to expel the 'barbarians'. But the Italian states, when they did form alliances, combined only so that when the common danger was past they could continue to differ. Florence had rejoiced when Naples had been conquered by foreigners in 1501, it gloated when Venice was stripped of its main land possessions by the 'barbarian' coalition of Cambrai in 1509. In a burst of literary enthusiasm in the last chapter of

able part of the European economy, indeed, depended on the pleasure taken in the feel of different stuffs, from furs to brocades, velvets and taffetas. Artists painted clothes with absorbed attention and some actually designed dress fabrics. The body, trained to the dance, adjusted itself with quick sympathy to weight and cut. Clothes were symbols of allegiance. Rulers dressed their servants in a uniform livery—red for the household of the Palatinate, scarlet and white for Aragon. Pope Leo X's musicians wore his white, red and green. The habit was repeated in noble households. Clothes were indicators of class, occupation and condition: virgin, wife or widow. All over Europe sumptuary legislation tried to curb sartorial extravagance in the interest of class harmony (the burgher's wife should not ape the noble's, nor the noble's flaunt her status), of decency (don't emphasise breasts or genitals), of morality (curb vanity and extravagance) and protectionism (don't buy imported materials). Constant repetition shows how impossible it was to check the appetite for variety and display.

Vain, too, were exhortations from the pulpit. 'Ladies', pleaded the Franciscan Michel Menot in a Lent sermon, 'in this time of penitence the church covers its saints with a veil; for the love of God do the same to your breasts.' On another occasion, 1508, he attacked the extravagance of their coiffures. 'O ladies, you who go in for finery, who often fail to listen to the word of God although you could do so by crossing the street, I am certain that it would take less time to clean out a stable of forty-four horses than it takes you to pin up you hair.' Vain were the laments of poets: in 1509 Alexander Barclay mourned that

'Man's form is disfigured with every degree,
As knight, squire, yeoman, gentleman and knave ...
Alas thus all estates of Christian men decline,
And of women also, disforming their figure.'

The pace at which fashions changed continued, indeed accelerated, with sleeves now wide as a monk's, now almost too tight to draw on, as another preacher complained in Stras-

and every inhabitant of the big commercial towns had at least a vague impression, as had those who possessed the many multi-lingual song books of the period.

Thanks to trade, diplomacy, the administration of multi-lingual realms and the employment of multi-lingual armies, a smattering of foreign languages was not an unusual accomplishment. Except among churchmen and at the universities, spoken Latin was becoming restricted to purely formal moments, like the presentation of an ambassador's letters of credence, or to bridge gaps in the understanding of a modern language. In his *Education of a Prince* (1518 or 1519), Budé stressed the importance of learning modern languages so that the ruler could endear himself to his various peoples and not be at the mercy of an interpreter. Maximilian jotted down his own achievements in a manuscript of his veiled autobiography, the *Weisskunig*: German as a child; Latin from the schoolmaster; Wendish and Bohemian from the peasants; French from his wife, Mary of Burgundy; Flemish from the circle of Margaret of York, Charles the Bold's widow; Spanish from diplomatic correspondence; Italian from army officers; English from archers in his pay. For diplomatic purposes King Manuel of Portugal learned Spanish and Henry VIII, with the aid of a resident tutor, learned French. Though the French were reluctant to learn other languages and, partly for this reason, their tongue was taking over from Latin as the major diplomatic language, Commines could carry on negotiations in Italian. Itinerant scholars, however passionately they felt about Latin, could not rely on it: Cornelius Agrippa learned French and Italian in addition to his native German. Purely as a polite accomplishment Lucrezia Borgia added French to the Spanish of her father's homeland and the Italian of her upbringing. The discoverers showed some interest in native tongues: a glossary of Malayan words was brought back by da Gama, and Pigafetta compiled one in Patagonian during his voyage with Magellan.

This accomplishment was seldom deep. The production of vernacular grammars, let alone dictionaries, was only beginning: the first thorough teaching aid was the Castilian gram-

German, and even then, when the first Low German translation of the bible was published in Cologne in 1479, it had to
have low Frankish and Low Saxon in parallel columns. More
confusing still was the situation in the Netherlands. In Antwerp, for instance, the language of local administration was
Flemish, of correspondence with the court or with the duke's
representatives French, of the ecclesiastical courts Latin, while
a swarm of translators aided commercial transactions in German, Italian and Spanish. In Russia there were three linguistic
divisions, Great Russian, Ukranian and Belorussian, but
travellers were as likely to be greeted in Church Slavonic as in
any of these. In Norway the ruling officials and most of the
merchants spoke Danish. There were tiny pockets in southern
Italy where Greek was still spoken, and the vernacular differences between the major states provided fuel for endless literary controversy. His own contribution to this controversy (*A
Dialogue on Language*), Machiavelli hoped, would establish
the primacy of Florence and 'disabuse those who are so un-
grateful for the benefits they have received from our city that
they are content to confound her language with those of Milan,
Venice and the Romagna, and with all the filthy usages of
Lombardy.'

Any impression of a foreign country was in any case still
further blurred by a stubborn folk-lore of phrases which purported to hit off national character in vivid shorthand. To the
German authors of the *Letters of Obscure Men* (1515–17) it
was axiomatic that Poland was the land of thieves, Bohemia
of heretics, Saxony of drunkards, Florence of homosexuals. In
this folk-lore the French were frivolous, Flemings were glut-
tons and preternaturally clean, the English foul-mouthed,
avaricious and insular; it was with no sense of discovery, but a
delight in spelling out a truism, that an Italian visitor to England explained that 'the English are great lovers of themselves,
and of everything belonging to them; they think that there are
no other men than themselves, and no other world but England; and whenever they see a handsome foreigner they say
that "he looks like an Englishman", and that "it is a great pity
that he should not be an Englishman"; and when they partake

In spite of the literary culture of Burgundy and the artistic achievements of the Netherlands, Italians clung to their conviction that north of the Alps Europe was in the hands of the barbarians. Writing to Leo X from sophisticated Brussels, Raphael's pupil Tommaso Vincidor complained 'I have much to bear, away among foreign barbarians.' Visiting the shrines of the Holy Land, Pietro Casola noted fastidiously that 'I always let the ultramontanes rush in front.' Christopher Scheurl angrily quoted in 1506 a Venetian saying that 'all the cities of Germany are blind—except Nuremberg, and that sees with only one eye!' On the other hand, 'we must make allowances', wrote Zwingli with lofty sarcasm, 'for Italian conceit . . . They cannot bear to see Germany out-stripping them in learning.' France, too, wished to import Italian culture uncontaminated by the Italian character. Singers from Milan had much to teach the Parisians, but Jean Marot could not forbear exclaiming that they sounded like the birth pangs of a nanny goat; they were also likened to piglets squealing in a sack. Learn from, but don't imitate: this was the message of Pierre Gringore's 'There is nothing worse, on my faith, than an Italianate Frenchman.'

Whether at the level of boys giving a tang to their games by playing French against Germans or of official propaganda, this moral chauvinism perhaps helped men to identify with international rivalries that were decided on solely by their rulers. But neither the phraseology of mutual recrimination, nor the awareness that other groups of men spoke different languages and wore different clothes, did much to bring about any clear sense of personal involvement with an individual's own country, let alone with Christendom as a whole.

iv

This sense of involvement was all the weaker because of the vigour of local associations and their ability to cater satisfactorily to the desire for mutual aid, spiritual fraternity, recreation and simple gregariousness.

sation and the overseeing of neighbourhood markets. The slow population recovery since the fourteenth century meant that most towns still retained large open spaces within the walls; in plan the town often resembled a group of villages, congregations of streets, of one or two storey houses for the most part, separated from the next nucleus by orchards or open spaces. This scattering of village-like districts was fostered by the police, customs and economic functions of the main gates which tended to become foci for inns, stables, markets and the shops and crafts dealing with the goods arriving along particular trade routes. The cathedral or largest church, and the town hall, exerted, of course a centralising pull, but even where the 'villages' blended into one another they preserved a warmly identifiable personality; with all classes working at home there was no morning or evening movement from one district to another. The tide might flow to the cathedral to hear a visiting preacher, to the town hall to listen to a proclamation, to a particular recreational area, but then it would flow back into the ward, to a self-contained and small-scale life, its homogeneity reflected in the inter-district rivalry of those horse races or football combats still commemorated in Italy.

Streets took their names from the trades practised in them, from local families and from local landmarks, church, brewery or inn, and shared occupational interest meant that kinsfolk usually lived in the same part of the town. Similarly, gild activity was frequently localised. There was no slackening of the social and economic purposes that had created the medieval gild. Constantly refurbishing their statutes to protect themselves from the 'foreigners' who were entering the towns in increasing numbers, they continued to care charitably for their members, to commission works of art for their chapels in the local church and to demonstrate that passion for their 'own' law which all occupation groups wished to preserve against the encroachments of municipal and royal legislation. The gilds represented an economic need, but the appetite for associations beyond such needs and beyond the circle of kin was stronger than ever. The *Meistersinger*, amateur musicians drawn from all trades, grew in numbers and enlarged their schools in the

of occultists, another group formed around the magician and mystic Mercurio da Correggio.

By means of such associations town life catered for business, religious, cultural and recreational interests. Conditions varied from town to town. Perhaps Venice was unique for the vivid role played by the gilds in the church festivals and state processions which made the Venetian calendar at once so formal and so gay. Nowhere else, perhaps, was there so much informed public interest as the Florentines showed in the great civic and gild commissions to painters, sculptors and architects. The extent of the control of the civic fathers over every detail of life, from the price of bread to the cut of clothes and the censorship of plays, was perhaps nowhere so complete as in the cities of Germany. But all towns offered a complex and satisfying system of relationships which left men with little inclination, save in the realm of business, to look outside to those larger and vaguer communities: the state, partnerships of states by alliance, Europe itself. In 1497 a traveller wrote of Calais: 'Every day in the afternoon, when the inhabitants take their rest, the gates are closed; and this also happens on holidays, only, instead of once, as on working days, it is done twice, the first time when services are being held in the churches, and a second time, as before, when the people are having lunch. At these times sentries and guards keep watch from the town's walls on all sides.' The town works, rejoices, takes its siesta like one huge, well-guarded family. In time of war the town's first thought was the defence of its walls. 'Politics' meant first and foremost civic politics, the elbowings and factions that can be suffered and seen. Pride was above all civic pride. The Parisians boasted of their new Pont-Notre-Dame, swinging easily over the Seine with its twenty-foot roadway and lines of shops; its cost of a quarter of a million *livres* was met more easily than any tax imposed by the state for a national purpose. In times of festival or when the entry of some great man was celebrated, a city could minister still further to this pride by appearing in disguise, fountains turned into stands for *tableaux vivants*, chariots of Love or Venus, or Death or Fortune, dragged by strange-costumed figures

as something to be achieved as easily within the context of the home as of the cloister. Respect for the familial *pietas* of ancient Rome coupled with distrust of monastic morals produced an idealisation of life in the family.

The solidarity of the family owed much to its being the centre of, not a retreat from, production. In the country the entire family worked on the land and, in winter, shared their home with the animals for the sake of their warmth. The craftsman worked in his own house, as did the shopkeeper. Servants and apprentices lived as members of the family segregated from the ordinary life of the household only by their duties. Under the partnership agreements that were common among French peasants different families lived under the same roof, all their property, down to kitchen utensils, being held in common. A more conscious feeling for family unity led to the production of household scenes in illumination, painting and woodcut, sometimes as backgrounds for, say, the Birth of the Virgin, but frequently as straightforward genre scenes. Servants ministered to masters with little sense of social divisiveness. Wife and husband ministered to one another as a necessity that might be affectionate and respectful even if it was rarely self-sufficient from the points of view of passion and understanding. The father was expected to rule, though his authority might be under heavy siege, and the atmosphere was gregarious; desire for privacy was still tentative (even in wealthy families very few girls had, as had Carpaccio's St. Ursula, a bedroom of their own).

The functional solidarity of the home makes it difficult to judge the quality, the emotional tone of family life. A high death rate meant frequent remarriages; not only were marriages planned by kinsmen and thus lacking, at least in the initial stages, in romance, but the speed with which a new marriage partner was brought into the home suggests a certain emotional casualness. Three successive marriages were common. Again, in wealthy families it was customary to send children out to a wet-nurse for the first months and also (though infrequently in Italy) to send them to be educated by growing up in some great household, a 'finishing' that began

part in the Italianising of Muscovite culture. The refinement
of the courts of Ferrara, Mantua and Urbino undoubtedly
owed much to the influence of a few highly educated women
like Isabella d'Este and Elisabetta Gonzaga. Born to rule, or
with the possibility of ruling, an Anne of Brittany or a Margaret of Austria could show herself the equal of men. By
chance the shopkeeper's daughter Sigbrit, mother of Christian
II of Norway's mistress, had an opportunity to show that a
shrewd bourgeoise could run a state better than a feeble king;
by chance a peasant girl, Maroula of Lemnos, showed that a
woman could rally a wavering garrison and lead it in a successful counter-attack against the Turks, an action for which
she was offered a dowry and the pick of an officer husband by
the Venetian state. Literature offered a few vivacious and
independent-minded heroines but for most writers, women's
place was firmly in the home, their interests restricted, as in
Fernando de Rojas' portrait, to ' "What did you have for dinner?" and "Are you pregnant?" and "How many chicks have
you got?" and "Take me to lunch at your house" and "Point
your lover out to me" and "How long is it since you saw
him?" and "How are you getting on with him?" and "What
are your neighbours like?" and other things like that.' Vespasiano da Bisticci, the Florentine bookseller and biographer,
would not even grant them this liberty. Women, he wrote,
should follow these rules: 'the first is that they bring up their
children in the fear of God, and the second that they keep
quiet in church, and I would add that they stop talking in
other places as well, for they cause much mischief thereby.'
The same note was sounded in England; 'there is nothing that
doth so commend, advance, set forth, adorn, deck, trim and
garnish a maid as silence', warned an anonymous English
tract. Among the patrons of William Caxton's printing press
was that vigorous woman Margaret Beaufort, Countess of
Richmond and Derby and co-founder of Christ's and St.
John's Colleges at Cambridge, but the printer described a
more passive ideal when he wrote that 'the women of this
country be right wise, pleasant, humble, discreet, sober,
chaste, obedient to their husbands, secret, steadfast, ever busy

in which a man and wife wrestled for who was to wear them; victory (sometimes determined by a delighted demon) usually went to the termagant wife. Other woodcuts and engravings dwelt alarmingly on famous cases of men being dominated by women: Adam tempted by Eve, Samson shorn by Delilah, Holofernes decapitated by Judith, Aristotle bridled and driven by Campaspe. The hen-pecked husband was a stock character in the drama. In a farce by Cuvier, Jacquinot's mother-in-law reminds him that he 'must obey his wife as a good husband should'. She and her daughter pen a lengthy list of his obligations and force him to sign it. He is to get up first, light the fires, prepare the breakfast, wash the children's soiled clothes, in fact 'come, go, run, trot, toiling away like Lucifer'. The dénouement comes, much to the relief of husbands in the audience, when his wife falls into an enormous wash-tub and begs him to pull her out. 'It's not on my list' is his answer to each plea, and he only rescues her in return for a promise that henceforward he will be master in his own house. This is caricature in humorous vein, but behind it is the fear of a darker form of domination, for this was a time when women were introduced into crucifixion plays gleefully forging the nails for the cross, and when a misericord could portray a woman heaving a man off to perdition with a rope round his genitals.

Fear of woman's sexuality appears to have been widespread. 'Where, alas!' sighed the foremost student of the printed sermon literature of late fifteenth century England, G. R. Owst, 'where is our merry medieval England?' The church, of course, drew on a long tradition in which woman was identified with *luxuria* and described in terms of pathological disgust. But it was not only clerics who believed, with Michel Menot, that 'luxuria etiam breves dies hominis facit'. Etienne Champier, a doctor as well as a poet, warned the readers of his *Livre de Vraye Amour* that too much lovemaking led to gout, anaemia, dyspepsia and blindness, and he was doing no more than repeat a medical commonplace. Both clerics and doctors reflected a fear that had its roots in the darkness of folk terrors. It was expressed in that most popular of travel books, the

(even if only a marginally viable one) by a series of voluntary restraints. One was postponement of marriage itself, for poor men frequently until between thirty and thirty-five. A second was making love in ways that could not lead to conception—ways in which the clergy were briefed to inquire about in the confessional and which they sought to combat. A third was abortion, again condemned, and, indeed, punishable with death, but common. The last recourse was exposure, and here, at least in the towns, foundling institutions accepted, wet-nursed and put out discarded infants to foster-parents, a system supported by a fairly general lack of social, if not legal, prejudice against the bastard. Thanks to these restraints and the high incidence of death due to disease, the average household probably did not number more than the parents and two or three children, though as kin usually lived in the same district, if not in the same street, this figure may conceal some redistribution of children among childless or slightly better-off relatives. Even so, it is difficult not to suspect that the confessions in witch trials involved a hysterical shifting of responsibility for the fantasies and aberrations caused by a fear-haunted sex-life, as did, in all probability, the accusations of sexual interference laid by men, with the assistance of celibate inquisitors, against the night-hags.

The contrast between precept and appetite was not only deep but open. Almost all the practices forbidden by the clergy can be illustrated in popular art, in books or in public entertainments. It was a mortal sin to take pleasure in watching the couplings of animals. In 1514 a widely publicised animal entertainment was put on in the Piazza dei Signori in Florence. Particularly noted was the moment when a mare was sent in among some stallions. In the opinion of one observer, the pious diarist Luca Landucci, 'this much displeased decent and well behaved people'. But in the eyes of another diarist, Cambi, it 'was the most marvellous entertainment for girls to behold.' Erasmus, in his very widely read *Colloquies*, takes lesbianism for granted as a hazard for young nuns, and among the popular stories attributed to Priest Arlotto Mainardi was one of a peasant who confessed not only to stealing the priest's corn

teased Willibald Pirckheimer about his taste for young men,
and Pomponius Laetus brushed off criticism of his homo-
sexuality with a reference to Socrates; yet preachers warned
the Italians that disaster after disaster, from the French invasion of 1494 to the Venetian earthquake of 1511, was a
punishment for sodomy. For many the black of conduct or
day-dream could apparently contrast with the white of
Christian teaching without strain, men turning easily from sin
to absolution, helped by a church which, realistically, was more
lenient in court and confessional than in the pulpit. But it is
clear that not all could accept this simple dualism, the tension
perceptible in sexual obsession was too apparent. In the course
of the French mystery play *The Vengeance and Destruction
of Jerusalem*, Nero orders an operation to be performed on
his mother so that he can see the precise place where he had
been conceived. Chastity belts were made, and shown in art,
even if they were not used. The tension inherent in the secular version of Christian morality worked out in the chivalrous
romance—in which there was a revival of interest at this
time—was shown by woodcuts spelling out the real object of
the heroes' worship. The mingling of sexual and devotional
imagery in the poetry of Skelton shows how that other ethe-
realisation of feeling for women, the literature of Mariolatry,
could be penetrated by imaginings of the grossest sort.

All this, of course, is evidence to be treated with great
caution. The fashion (in some places) for low cut dresses and
(mainly in Germany) for codpieces of aggressive cut and
colour tells us little: it is impossible to recapture the emotional effect of a past fashion. Similiarly, we can draw no conclusion from the proliferation of the lifelike nude in art. Sug-
gestiveness has little to do with realism. Besides, the nude
could still draw on a tradition which associated it with shame
or humility: it was in this guise that Memling painted Tommaso Portinari kneeling naked, his wife beside him, in the
scales of judgement. We may doubt, however, if anyone took
sex as neutrally as the Utopians, among whom it was lumped
with the comparable off-hand pleasures of scratching and de-
faecating.

tonio de Beatis wrote of the young Francis I that 'although of such slight morals that he slips readily into the gardens of others and drinks the waters of many fountains, he treats his wife with much respect and honour.' Johann Cuspinians's eulogy of the Emperor Maximilian stressed that 'unlike other princes' he was always virtuous in his relations with women. This double standard of morality was not peculiar to princes, and that it was avenged is shown by prints in which the lover slips from the bedroom as the husband enters. The Utopians were anxious guardians of sexual morality. 'The reason why they punish this offence so severely,' More explained, 'is their fore-knowledge that, unless persons are carefully restrained from promiscuous intercourse, few will contract the tie of marriage, in which a whole life must be spent with one companion, and all the troubles incidental to it must be patiently borne.'

It is not surprising that prostitution flourished, government and, much more grudgingly, the church, seeing it as an essential safety valve. Recruitment was kept up by poverty, especially in times of dearth when families could only survive by prostituting their daughters. The demand was maintained by population figures that point to a considerable imbalance between the sexes, men being well in the majority. There were (unreliable) estimates of 6,800 for the prostitutes of Rome in 1490 and 11,000 for those of Venice in the early sixteenth century. Their regulation differed according to the views of the municipal authorities. Coquillart represents the streets of Paris haunted by a familiar figure: 'Woman who goes torchless by night. And murmurs to each "do you want me?"' while in Nuremberg prostitutes, though protected by statutes of their own, were required to stay in state-licensed brothels. The introduction of syphilis made little difference to this open mindedness; caution, not panic, was the main reaction. It was indeed during this period that the prostitute came into her own. The substitution of the word 'courtesan' for 'sinner' reflects a growing tolerance for the profession as a whole, and in Italy, and especially in Rome, the prostitute catered for romantic companionship as well as lust. From the home then, men

death shall have annihilated us.'

Generally, however, a messenger's verbal report meant more than the letter he carried, the gift for expressing spontaneity in writing being uncommon. The ability to sustain a relationship by correspondence was rare; men liked to see and jostle one another, to drink and pray and argue and conduct business together. What they could not see and hear they found difficult to imagine, and any discussion of governmental changes, foreign relations and war must take this into account.

than many areas polarised towards the few which trafficked on
a large scale with the lands then in process of discovery.

The exploitation of these lands had, indeed, proceeded at a
remarkable pace, By 1515, the end of the Portuguese viceroy
Affonso d'Albuquerque's period of office, fleets were returning
regularly from the west Indian coasts, protected as they
assembled by the fortified ports of Diu, Goa and Cochin and
from Arab raiders on their way across the Indian Ocean by
ships based on Ormuz and Mombasa. A fort at Malacca, moreover, acted as a forward base for the continuing exploration
of Malaysia and the Moluccas. Before Cortes landed in Mexico
in 1519 Spain had established settlements in the West Indies
in Santo Domingo, Jamaica, Cuba and Puerto Rico and was
building Darien, in Colombia, into the first Spanish town on
the mainland. As yet, however, it is doubtful whether either
of the great colonising powers made more out of their overseas empires than they put into them. Much of the capital for
the voyages was raised from Italian and German bankers,
who had to be repaid. Portuguese spices brought an initial
profit to Lisbon, but as they were increasingly forwarded to
Antwerp for distribution the retail profit fell to non-Portu-
guese hands. And though enough gold was coming to Spain
from the West Indies to begin the rise in prices that was to
infect Europe as a whole by the end of the century, Spain's
real wealth was to come from the silver mines of South
America which were as yet undiscovered. The European
economy was only marginally affected by the consequences of
the voyages of Columbus and da Gama by 1520.

The direction of the flow of basic foodstuffs and raw
materials in Europe remained constant: flax and furs moving
westwards from Poland and Lithuania, Sicilian grain and
cotton moving northwards, wool from Spain and England
moving eastwards, and salt fish moving south from the Baltic
and the North sea. The areas of dense population and of manufacture, the chief absorbers of these commodities, did not
shift; the centre of gravity of Europe's financial and industrial
life continued to be the southern Netherlands and north-
eastern France, south Germany and northern Italy. The Rhine,

A multitude of seigneurial rights and municipal privileges came between the producer and the consumer. Attempts were made to improve roads as an alternative to the use of rivers especially burdened with tolls; in France associations of merchants were formed to bargain with riparian landlords. But transport costs continued to determine prices, and therefore wages. It was, again, transport costs that maintained the essentially regional nature of economic activity, with small market towns serving and being served by hinterlands with a radius of fifteen to twenty miles; transport costs that ensured that apart from raw materials, like wool, and basic foodstuffs, grain, oil, salt and wine, long distance commerce catered almost exclusively for the rich. With the possible exception of a single outfit of holiday clothing, it is doubtful whether the great majority of men possessed any object whose maker they were not in a position to know personally. Because of distribution costs merchants strove, in the teeth of governmental regulations, to establish monopolies, the great trading companies to increase their profits in rare but essential commodities like copper and alum by establishing cartels. Nor did the basic characters of large firms alter in other respects. They played safe by diversifying their interests as had their medieval predecessors, combining banking with commerce and industry, and they continued to make loans to princes in exchange for trading privileges: the Hansa helped Edward IV to the throne of England, the Fuggers and Welsers paid for the electoral votes that gave Charles V an empire.

While the basic conditions of economic life remained stable there were, of course, regional changes. The rapid development of Icelandic fishing grounds at the expense of those of the Baltic damaged the prosperity of Bergen, which had been for centuries based on the salting and re-distribution of herring and cod. The shortage of precious metals for coin, especially for purchases in the Levant and the Indies and, on a lesser scale, for the payment of armies, led to a notable development of the silver mines in Saxony and Bohemia and made the fortunes of the firms which managed them. The old silver mining towns of Saxony increased at a rate that radically altered the

left but a painful bruise and not a permanent gash on this arm of Venetian trade. In 1504 Portuguese spices were on sale in London, and in the same year Venetian galleys found none at either of the two chief spice outlets in the Mediterranean, Alexandria and Beirut—ports at which they were accustomed to finding three million pounds weight or more. The shock of these first years, and the panic that accompanied it, did not last long. The empty quays were the result not of Portuguese monopoly but of the temporary dislocation of the Arab distribution service across the Indian ocean to the Red Sea and the Persian Gulf: not the holds but the guns of Portuguese ships were to blame. By the beginning of the 1520s the links with Arab distributors had been re-established. Henceforward Venetian spices had to compete with those of Lisbon, but the purchase price at both ports was roughly the same and the demand was higher than ever. Spices (chiefly pepper) were only one of the commodities handled by Venetian shipping, though they were the most valuable. Apart from importing other eastern luxury goods the city and its *terra ferma* had begun slowly but profitably to weave cloth. The production of glassware and printed books was increased. This diversity, plus the resumption of spice imports, led to Venice's being more prosperous in the 1520s than it had been during the 1480s. War with the Turks from 1499–1502, the news from Lisbon, bank failures and heavy subsidies to allies, shattering defeat at Agnadello in 1509: Venice weathered all these crises. It was in these years that the process of converting the wooden bridges over the canals into stone ones was begun. The Fondaco dei Tedeschi, burned down in 1505, was at once rebuilt on a grander scale than ever, as was the district on the other side of the Rialto when in 1514 it, too, was destroyed by fire.

Changes did occur in the respective importance of cities and firms as well as of whole regions. Freer trading practices and protection pushed Antwerp well ahead of its old rival Bruges. The international fairs at Lyons continued to draw business away from those of Geneva. Amsterdam became one of the busiest fishing ports in northern Europe, largely at the expense of the Baltic ports. Even more dramatic was the ex-

proclaiming that 'he would not be satisfied unless he had secured 5,000 *cruzados* and many pearls and rubies within the space of three years.'

On the other hand, Dürer was drawing on widespread condemnations of idleness when he engraved a bourgeois sleeping by a stove, his coffer closed, and dreaming, under the influence of the devil, not of profit but of Venus. The Venetian diarist Girolamo Priuli ascribed a similarly non-militant posture not to the devil but to a resting on economic laurels. 'Our ancestors were brave, fierce, impatient of injuries, quick to strike, prone to fight. Now we are of milder mind, meek, long-suffering, shy of a blow, shrinking from war. And this, I take it, because in olden times we all lived by trading and not on fixed incomes; we spent many years of our lives in distant lands, where we dealt with different races and grew courageous ... Now few of us live by trade. Most subsist on their incomes or on their official pay.'

For Priuli, then, the soldiering age was over. He spoke of Venice, but there was a widespread increase in the number of *rentiers* and those who aspired to the security of administrative office. Indeed, with the possible exception of Antwerp, where a local boom led to an intense competitiveness among the swelling foreign communities and native traders, it is easier to see the bourgeoisie as above all cautious in business, with a strong sense of duty and obligation to civic affairs, distrustful of new ideas and genuinely religious. 'And since our Lord God is the giver of every good', runs a passage in a Florentine parnership agreement of 1506, 'they are agreed that of the said profits of this firm, they shall give every Sunday as alms to orphan children 2 florins for every 100 florins they have received during the week, either as a firm, or else each member himself shall distribute according to this rule.' Far more representative than Jacob Fugger's remark is the tone caught by Luca Pacioli in his statement that 'the purpose of every merchant is to make a lawful and reasonable profit so as to keep up his business.'

There were, in any case, few areas of economic activity which held out the temptation to get very rich very fast. The

at the university of Ingolstadt, argued at a debate in Bologna in 1515 that a trading loan could properly carry five per cent interest (the Fugger banking firm had paid his travelling expenses), his friend Pirckheimer, himself scion of a wealthy merchant family, wrote 'it pains me to see you meddling with a subject that cannot but stain your conscience', and he warned Eck that he was merely being used for propaganda purposes.

Neither the direct prohibitions of canon law, nor a steady stream of pulpit reprimand, had succeeded in stopping economic self-interest from using the loan, or trading for the maximum profit that could be obtained. Sometimes the convention was blandly ignored. In Russia it was the monasteries which were the pacemakers in business techniques; in certain towns, like Geneva, the authorities, albeit with certain qualifications, legitimised loans involving interest; in Lyons merchants were allowed to charge 15 per cent in deals among themselves. Most frequently it was sidestepped by fictions: a loan was disguised as an investment or a partnership, or, rather more baldly, repayment sums which concealed the interest involved were named in contracts, or loans were repaid in foreign currency, thus representing an exchange or reciprocal purchase. Or a bank would pay what amounted to interest in the form of an annual gift; as long as expressions of gratitude to the depositor were not a condition of the deposit no infringement of canon law was involved, indeed, as the bank might go up in flames, or the money, invested by the banker in, say, a trading fleet, might go to the bottom, the depositor was facing a conjectural risk and was entitled to some compensatory payment. All these devices were already familiar by the fourteenth century. It is doubtful whether the usury laws had any effect whatsoever on economic productivity in Europe as a whole, but they possibly affected the channels into which economic activity was directed, and they did provide a climate of opinion to which the individual had to adjust with varying degrees of comfort. As the most straightforwardly wicked interest-bearing loan was one made to a consumer who found himself in financial straits, and the church was more tolerant to loans (as long as there was no named, fixed interest rate)

unlucky clergy either became permissive or shifted their responsibility by applying for rulings to the university of Paris.
Uneasiness about the moral status of the business life was
probably at its most perturbed in the first generation of the
sixteenth century. The edgy religiosity which was a characteristic of this period had something to do with it. In addition,
the first tremors of what was to be a widespread rise of prices
faced the consumer with a phenomenon which, in the absence
of realistic economic theory, he put down to the wicked
machinations of business men, to *Fuggerei*. And with the rise
in prices came a ripple of extra profits available for re-invest-
ment, thus drawing still sharper attention to the breeding of
money by money.

It was, of course, possible to make a fortune in business,
to move from rags to riches, but such careers were made
against a prevailing wind of unadventurous protectionism.
State intervention was hamstrung between a bullionist impulse
to cut imports and stimulate home production on the one
hand, and on the other a desire to damp down luxury consumption and keep the prices of basic consumables and
foodstuffs low. Nor, among municipal bodies, was there any
change in the medieval assumption that the duty of the city
fathers was to keep prices down and quality high. Towns pro-
liferated with inspectors of meat and poultry, measurers of
cloth, testers of wine and beer and bread, assayers of jewellery.
This did not conflict with the mood of most producers. The
general trend in Europe was for gild organisations, whether
self-governing or responsible to king or town council, to deny
any impulse to freedom of trade or manufacture, to become
monopolistic and to make the master-apprentice-journeyman
system more rigid. In Amiens, where the number of crafts
which hardened into gilds increased from twelve in 1400 to
forty-two in 1500, the Sisters of Mercy were forbidden to
make goods to sell for the benefit of their charitable funds. The
age of the all-round man was also the age in which the hilts,
the blades and the sheaths of swords were made by different
gilds, when a saddle was the work of three separate crafts: the
wooden frame made by one, the padding added by another,

as part-time bankers through the manipulation of loans. It was
here that the greatest opportunities lay, together with the
greatest risks, and it is because circumstances were encouraging the differences between these two chief types of bourgeois
activity that no easy definition of the urban middle and upper
classes can do justice to the variety of their lives and aims.

Even among the supreme opportunities, however, it took
more than one generation to bring about a significant change
in a family's purchasing power and the esteem in which it was
held, and it was above all a combination of mercantile wealth
and administrative position which produced the most dramatic
examples of mobility from one social environment clear into
another. The career of Jacques de Beaune is conspicuous almost to the point of caricature. Son of a moderately well-to-do
merchant, he married into the circle of royal officials, and
helped by these connections and the skill with which he
multiplied his fortunes as merchant and banker, he became
purveyor of plate to the crown, treasurer to Queen Anne and,
in 1495, receiver general for Languedoc. Having inherited
3,112 *livres* on his father's death, by the end of the century
he was worth more than 100,000 and by 1518 was able to
lend the crown 240,000 for building operations at the
châteaux of Amboise and Plessis-les-Tours. Ennobled by
Louis XII in 1510, he received the barony of Semblançay in
1515 from the Queen Mother, Louise of Savoy, whose financial affairs he administered in addition to his receivership.
Meanwhile his personal business concerns continued to prosper and a succession of gifts flowed from the individuals and
towns he dealt with in his official capacity. In 1523 he reached
the peak of his career. Already one of the richest men in
France he became, as *trésorier de l'épargne*, the chief financial
officer of the kingdom. Four years later, after proven charges
of peculation, he was hanged.

Finally, little if any challenge to re-thinking the ways in
which money could be made came from the business community itself, or from mathematic or applied science. There was
no important change in business techniques. Already by the

ing of the psychology of the business man, was the widespread retention of Roman numerals for calculation in preference to Arabic ones; time, space and accuracy were all sacrificed to this prejudice. Vagueness and confusion about numbers was responsible for much mercantile and agrarian litigation, but even the highest reaches of accounting practice were not exempt. Roger Doucet, editor of the financial records of the French crown for 1523, has pointed out that 'errors in calculation are to be taken for granted. An accurate addition sum is the exception. The errors are often considerable, sometimes beyond the order of one hundred thousand *livres*.'

The trader's life was complicated by the multitude of different coins. Pacioli mentioned only a few of those in common use in Italy: Venetian ducats, papal, Sienese and Florentine florins, *troni*, *marcelli*, papal and Neapolitan *carlini*, Florentine *grossi* and the *testoni* of Milan. The situation was worsened by the fact that as none of these coins was milled they could be clipped or filed by unscrupulous dealers. They were, moreover, beaten out and impressed not by machine but by hammer strokes: the thickness was therefore variable. A further difficulty was the variety of units of measurement, from 'the iron yard of our lord the King' in England to the numerous *passi* of Italy. It is true that these complications were taken in the merchant's stride; he valued coins by weight, there were printed tables for the conversion of measures, and he had measuring sticks for the units most commonly used for the goods he handled, but constantly weighing, measuring, handling for quality, performing calculations with counters on a squared board or cloth: a plethora of sense impressions appears to have inhibited more than a most elementary use of mental arithmetic by the merchant and possibly explains the retention of Roman numerals with its consequent toll of errors. Just as in medicine there was little contact between the theoretical teaching of the universities and practical doctoring, so the mathematics (mainly geometry) of higher education offered no lessons to men engaged in trade.

There was a similar gap between university-based science and everyday technology. To the Turks, Europe was a huge

and planets revolving round the earth, but which told the time indifferently, or multi-barrelled pistols, or crossbow- and pike-gun combinations, technically fascinating but well-nigh useless weapons.

Then, as Roland Mousnier has pointed out*, there was a widespread inability to learn from experience. He instances the agricultural practice of Poitou, where crops sown on land where chalk outcrops were ploughed into the soil yielded particularly well. Yet there was no attempt to mix chalk with the soil elsewhere, even though this was well within the technical competence of the farmers in the area. Finally, there was almost no flow of ideas, in any direction, between science, technological ingenuity, and craft or industrial experience.

Industrial plants were too small to present a challenge to the organising power of the capitalists and managers who ran them or to tempt them to look outside traditional ways of working. The industry which employed the largest number of workers, the making of cloth, involved something like twenty stages between the raw wool and the final product. Only two of these stages involved the use of anything that resembled a factory where large numbers of men worked together: fulling, done in large yards, and tentering (stretching), which was carried out on simple frames in long sheds, as was the plaiting and tensioning of rope. The other stages were carried out on a family or group basis. The organisation required was a fairly simple matter of timetable and transport; the investment in plant, and therefore the attention paid to equipment, was tiny compared with the money sunk in raw material and wages.

The largest industrial plant in Europe was the Venetian Arsenal or shipbuilding yard, which employed some 4,000 workers in busy years. In some years the alum works at Tolfa, in the Papal States, employed even more, but with the failure of the Volterra supplies at the end of the fifteenth century and the collapse of French attempts to process their own deposits at a reasonable price, Tolfa remained the sole example of this

* In *Études sur la France de 1494 à 1559* (Cours de Sorbonne, Paris, n.d.) 38–9.

iii

The extent to which governments intervened in the business affairs of individuals and corporations varied, but all did intervene and all had the same objectives, to encourage native products and protect them from foreign competition, and to prevent the flow of bullion abroad by making their countries as self-supporting as possible. The economic element in nationalism was the first to be widely appreciated and acted upon.

Because the French linen industry was languishing and Frenchmen were importing the fabric from England, Italy and Spain, Louis XI encouraged the linen producers of Arras, Rheims and elsewhere by granting tax concessions to the towns concerned and by increasing the import duties on the foreign cloth. His successor forced the other trades in Poitiers to give subsidies to the linen industry until it was back on its feet. To encourage the iron industry, Louis exempted miners and smelters from taxation and compelled local landowners to supply iron-masters with timber for fuel. Maritime governments commonly offered subsidies to firms building merchant ships large enough to be converted into fighting vessels in time of war; though this was a way of getting a navy on the cheap it was also in line with laws, like the Castilian edict of 1500, which required a nation's goods to be exported in native shipping. In addition to customs dues, a further means of cutting down imports was the use of sumptuary laws forbidding the wearing of foreign products. To give an example for the observation of these laws, no Venetian public official was permitted to wear cloth that had not been made in Venice or its *terra ferma*. In a (vain) attempt to protect the Catalan coral industry, which produced ornaments much prized abroad, it was forbidden to export the special tools which would have made coral working easier for others. Government action could determine the economic prosperity of individual towns. The choice of Calais as sole export outlet for English wool is one example, the sacrifice of other towns

the *consulado* of Burgos which made that city the funnel into
which all Castilian wool ran before being exported to northern
Europe. In 1503, following this model, the *Casa de contrata-
cion* was established in Seville as the sole receiving and
distribution point for goods from the Americas. But the most
dramatic of these sleeping partnerships, whereby the crown
channelled commerce through its own pocket, was contracted
with the *Mesta*, the association of Castilian sheep farmers. The
flocks were of enormous size, some three million in all. Because of the nature of the country they were moved from
mountain pasture in the winter to summer grazing in the
plains over distances of as much as four hundred and fifty
miles. Along the routes they followed there was a natural conflict of interests. Agriculturalists wanted to increase the amount
of land put down to corn, vines and olives, all commodities in
high demand, the sheep owners wanted huge corridors of
pasturage. From 1489 Ferdinand and Isabella published a
series of edicts in the interest of the *Mesta*, of which the most
important, issued in 1501, guaranteed to members the undisputed tenancy of lands on which flocks had been pastured in
the past, regardless of any subsequent change of intention on
the part of the owner of the land. Others secured shepherds
against imprisonment as securities for the debts of their employers and exempted them from military service. Another,
sacrificing the oldest of crown monopolies to its most recent
monopolistic *protégé*, exempted the *Mesta* from the tax on the
loads of salt which accompanied the flocks.

How far this descent of the crown into the market place was
prompted by governmental initiative and how far by requests
from merchants and manufacturers is difficult to say, but it
sprang from the very naturalness of an interplay between
government and production. When Louis XI, after consulta-
tion with manufacturers, published an ordinance in 1479 (repeated and elaborated in 1512) which regulated the quality,
the number of threads and the length per piece of cloth for
the area within the jurisdiction of the *parlements* of Paris,
Rouen, Bordeaux and Toulouse, he was simply carrying out a
function at a national level which had habitually been carried

straightforward methods of clearance, Lisbon became the tightest bottleneck in Europe; the pioneer exploring country also pioneered the constricting use of red tape. Spain provides a third example of the hazards faced by the move towards overall planning. After the union of the crowns of Aragon and Castile, the advanced gild structure of Aragonese crafts was, in the interest of uniformity and of convenience, introduced into Castile, thus constricting rather than encouraging production there. Favour shown to the *Mesta* at the expense of arable farming led to a socially perilous rise in the price of foodstuffs. Cumulatively, these factors were even more disadvantageous to the country's economy than the expulsion of the Jews, whose economic role was gradually taken over by foreigners.

All plans to use government as an instrument of economic change were hampered by a lack of trained bureaucratic specialists. Above all they were hampered by unmethodically kept records and inadequate statistics. Governments could only guess at what would happen in the future because they had no clear figures which showed what had happened in the past. At a time when there was considerable vagueness as to a country's population, let alone its trade balances, when generals could misjudge the number of men under their command by as much as one third, when even Venice, a business state run by business men, could build more galleys than it could possibly man—when these errors in calculation are taken into account, a hit-or-miss element in commercial plans must be taken for granted.

The same is true of fiscal plans. The idea of an annual budget, a balance between national income and expenditure, was by now commonplace, as were attempts to forecast expenditure in the coming year. In small countries, especially where the tax burden fell predominantly on one large city, as in the case of Florence, a balance could be struck with some regularity, though it was never possible to estimate it at any time between the major audits. In large countries like France, it was seldom that the returns from outlying administrative districts turned up in time to make the annual balance com-

led nobles to refuse to pay taxes because their swords and their blood were permanently on offer to government, and clerics grudged serving a country with taxes because they were already serving it with their prayers (they were in fact taxed separately from laymen, and more lightly). At the end of the fifteenth century, when the Milanese came temporarily under French rule, the city council of Piacenza refused to pay excise duties because of an extraordinary rumour that in France— probably the most heavily taxed nation in Europe—no one paid taxes unless he chose to. In France itself another tradi- tion—by now so outmoded as to be hardly more than a super- stition—that the king could live on the income from his own domains alone was taken perfectly seriously by the estates general of 1484. In all monarchies a distinction was made between ordinary revenue, the personal income of the king, and extraordinary revenue in the form of taxes, duties and loans. Henry VII, whose personal income was reorganised and exploited with some thoroughness, still needed the export duty on wool and leather and the import and export duties on wine even in years of peace. Indeed, government everywhere was becoming a more expensive business but, except in the case of war, it was difficult for the taxpayer to see why this was so, and this was another element in the reluctance to pay.

Addressing the young Charles of Habsburg, who, as the Emperor Charles V, was to be Europe's greatest taxmaster, Erasmus took it for granted that a king would try to live with- out taxing his subjects unless 'some taxation is absolutely necessary and the affairs of the people render it essential.' In that case he should penalise the rich and tax 'the extravagant luxuries and delicacies which only the wealthy enjoy', among which he named jewels, silk, spices and dyes. For 'a good prince will tax as lightly as possible those commodities which are used by the poorest members of society, e.g. grain, bread, beer, wine, clothing and all the other staples without which human life could not exist...But it so happens that these very things bear the heaviest tax in several ways; in the first place, by the oppressive extortion of the tax farmers ..., then by import duties which call for their own set of extortionists,

Roses meant that many estates could be shown to have escheated to the crown for lack of heirs. Heirs who were minors were declared wards of the crown, which administered their lands and took its profits until they came of age— at which point they paid a livery fee to take up their inheritance. Henry VIII, in a notable stroke of legal archaeology, persuaded parliament to accept his levy of feudal aids for the knighting of his eldest son and on the marriage of his eldest daughter.

The example of England shows how effective a bait was held out to fiscal efficiency and centralisation by the possibility of increasing revenue. In the reign of Henry VII alone, income from crown lands, customs duties, feudal rights, and legal fees and penalties almost tripled from about £52,000 to some £142,000 a year. In France, too, the income from crown lands was increased as well as the national revenue as a whole. But increased efficiency did not include taking stock of the social effects of a system which included, indeed was based on, the faults to which Erasmus drew attention. Unlike England, the French government relied heavily on a permanent extraordinary tax, the *taille*, an income tax which produced something like 83 per cent (in 1483) of the total revenue. As nobles, the clergy, judges and many other officials, together with certain towns, were exempt from this, the burden fell on the classes least able to bear it, especially on the peasantry. In addition, sales taxes (*aides*) were not only imposed on luxuries like silk, spices, dyes and jewellery, but on almost the whole range of staples: wine, grain, meat, poultry and fish, on woollen goods and shoes, on building materials and on coal and charcoal. Again, the poor were hardest hit. This inequity, least noticeable in England but characteristic of all European governments, was not only socially hazardous and involved formidable collection costs, it also encouraged evasion and smuggling.

In general, then, old methods were improved and in some cases extended, but there was no radical re-thinking of fiscal policy. Nor were governments able to keep the whole process of revenue collecting in their own hands. Lacking sufficient

# CHAPTER V

# CLASS

i

Between 1515 and 1519 Nicolas Manuel painted for the Dominicans of Bern a Dance of Death which reflects the number of categories into which an intelligent townsman divided his social world. The church was represented by pope, cardinal, patriarch, bishop, abbot, canon, monk and hermit; noble blood by emperor, king, duke, count, knight and a member of the Teutonic Order; commoner blood by an academic and a practising doctor, a jurist and an advocate, an astrologer, a councillor, a rich merchant and one of lesser standing, a magistrate, a bailiff, a soldier, a peasant, an artisan, a cook and a painter. Death came to interrupt the occupations of each of them, as he did to take away an empress, a queen, an abbess, a nun and a prostitute and five allegorical figures: girl, wife, widow, bachelor and madman.

Conservatives still saw society as divided into three mutually-supporting estates. Caxton's *Mirror of the World* (1481) put the traditional formula of the commons who work, the knights who fight and the clergy who pray, in its simplest form. 'The labourers ought to provide for the clerks and knights such things as were needful for them to live by in the world honestly; and the knights ought to defend the clerks and the labourers that there were no wrong done to them; and the clerks ought to instruct and teach these two manner of people, and to address them in their works in such wise that none do [any] thing by which he should displease God nor lose His grace.' This ideal of harmony and balance was popularised through the commonplace analogies of the day: society existed in terms of three estates as God existed within the Trinity; the game of chess depended on the King being supported by knights, bishops and com-

ducers, peasants and artisans, but includes petty officials, merchants in a small way of business and the lower ranks in the army. It is an inferior, a dependent estate 'according to reason and political necessity, just as in the human body there must be inferior organs, the servants of those of higher worth and dignity.' Tropes aside, and granting the influence of the medieval preoccupation with triads, the Seyssel formula was in accord with reality. And an added note of observation is given in a chapter 'How one moves from the third to the second, and from the second to the first estate' in which Seyssel explains that ambition can lead a commoner to prosper his way into the second estate, and outstanding public service can lead the king to ennoble members of the second estate into the first, whose ranks are, in any case, constantly shrinking thanks to death in war and, a significant point, poverty. This mobility, he notes, acts as an essential safety valve: without it 'those whose ambition is irrepressible would conspire with other members of their estate against those above them.' As it is, mobility is such that 'every day one sees members of the popular estate mount by degrees into that of the nobility and numberless into the middle estate.' And being a man of his times, for whom observation was not enough, he added that this reproduced Roman practice, whereby plebeians could rise to become knights and proceed to the patrician class.

The distinction between aristocratic blood on the one hand and, on the other, varying degrees of wealth was regularly made by governments in their tax and social legislation. The English sumptuary regulations of 1517, for instance, were designed to cut down extravagance and ostentation in the giving of meals, and clerics were included. The noble categories were: cardinal (nine dishes per meal); archbishop and duke (seven); marquis, earl, bishop (also seven); lords temporal under the degree of earl, abbots being in the House of Lords, mayors of the city of London, Knights of the Garter (six). The others were allowed, according to goods possessed or to income, five, four or three dishes. And 'it is ordered that in case any of the estates or other before rehearsed shall fortune to dine or sup with any other of a lower degree, it shall be

as responsible to Rome, as celibates, as administrators of the sacraments and as butts of an inclusive anticlericalism, presented the appearance of a separate order scattered through, but essentially different from the rest of society.

Where the formula really broke down was over the third estate. With municipal corporations, law merchant, gilds, confraternities, different procedures for free and unfree tenures, the third estate was broken up into occupations, interest and status groups even in the eye of the law. In representative bodies, from the English parliament to the Catalan *cortes* or the Bohemian diet, the third estate covered a broad social spectrum, from middling merchants to widely-acred gentlemen. In practice no one felt 'part of' the third estate but part of a specific occupational group, and, within that, of a specific income group. When polemicists, preachers or satirists looked round for social targets they attacked the nobility as a whole, the clergy usually under two heads, bishops and parish priests, and monks and friars, and the third estate in terms of a number of groups which were felt to practice a way of life that distinguished them from others. Cornelius Agrippa, in his *De vanitate*, attacked merchants (cheats and usurers), lawyers shysters) and doctors (quacks) before passing to a blanket condemnation of the poor (stupid, superstitious, crude). Olivier Maillard, preaching in 1500 in Bruges, singled out princes and courtiers, then officials, merchants and lawyers. In his *Ship of Fools* (1494) Sebastian Brant attacked artisans,

> *Every apprentice would be a master,*
> *For all the trades a great disaster,*

lawyers, doctors

> *And while he thumbs the folios*
> *The patient to the bone-yard goes,*

merchants and their wives

> *A burgher's wife now often wears*
> *Clothes better than a countess bears,*

cenary soldiers. Either because of itinerancy, or novelty, or changing attitudes to their social position, these groups did not fit easily into any stratified view of the third estate; nor did such a view take note of Jews, gypsies or slaves.

Complicating this already imprecise impression was one overriding prejudice, stronger probably than the barrier to sympathy between layman and priest; the townsman's prejudice against the countryman. Yet it is not as though rural and urban life were out of touch with one another. From Lisbon to Moscow vegetables were grown within the walls and the citizen relied on milk and meat from his own cows. The city fathers of Frankfurt-am-Main had to pass an ordinance forbidding citizens to keep pigsties on the street side of their houses and in other German towns wine growers and market gardeners formed special gilds. In Dijon artisans—furriers, carpenters, coopers and others—had vineyards and sold what wine they did not consume themselves. And if country occupations were a commonplace in the towns, the need for many countrymen to have two sources of income brought town occupations to the country, spinning, weaving, nail-making; most of the craftsmen who brought their baskets, saddlery, pots and pans to local markets were seasonal agriculturalists. Apart from the small merchant and the town-based bailiff or steward, few tradesmen moved about far in the country, but towns received a steady drift of farm labourers in search of work. There was interchange higher up the social scale: the yeoman's son who settled in a town, and whose family moved back to the country after two or three prosperous generations, was not an uncommon phenomenon. The majority of nobles, though they might have a town house and spend some time following the court, passed most of their lives on their country estates, were familiar with every detail of the agricultural year and were led by hawk and hound through every rural scene.

Yet for all these contacts there was an emotional gulf between town and country dweller, narrowest among the rich, widest when all other classes contemplated that universal butt, the peasant, most pungently expressed in the most highly

Saturne'.*

This antagonism drew on centuries during which towns had bargained and fought their way to some measure of self-government against church, noble and monarch and had thrown off the taint of servility that still clung to the country-side. And as the standard of living and the level of education in the towns grew, the contrast of manners came to constitute another barrier; More had his Utopian citizens educated in the country and forced to return to agricultural tasks from time to time in order to break it down.

The burden of satire—'All lands into disgrace have got, And none's contented with his lot'—is that this was a period of vigorous social change, of scrambling competitive-ness. When searching for the psychological causes of war, civil faction and popular disturbances, historians almost unani-mously pitched on ambition as the prime mover. Wherever we turn we find complaints that men are not content with the con-ditions in which they have been bred. 'The people have taken on airs', wrote the Lyons chronicler Symphorien Champier, 'and entertained evil ideas ... and the servants, who once were humble in the presence of their masters and were sober and poured much water into their wine ... now wish to drink better wine, like their masters, without any water or admixture what-soever, which is a thing against all reason.' Handbooks for con-fessors admonished the clergy to warn their parishioners against envying the possessions or social position of others and not to eat or dress above their station. Clichthove complained in ser-mon after sermon about congregations who treated the church as an extension of the market place, passing contracts about and discussing business deals. A German preacher described in 1515 a world that seemed to him to have gone money mad. 'Everyone thinks he will grow rich and put his money out to the best advantage. The artisan and the peasants invest their money in a company, or with tradesmen. They think to gain a great deal, and, often they lose everything. This evil did not exist in former times; it has grown up in the last ten years.' In

* Elizabeth Armstrong, *Ronsard and the age of gold* (Cambridge U.P., 1968) 3.

in their canton voted to raise money to provide the French with troops. But in general there was no class antagonism in the sense of one class wishing permanently to dispossess another.

> *When Adam dug and Eve span*
> *Who was then the gentleman?*

lingered on as a slogan, not a policy. Among the lowest ranks there was insufficient strength, among the moderately well-to-do sufficient upwards mobility, to ensure that social pressures were for the most part contained within the various compartments of the hierarchy of wealth and honour. The poor, especially the poor immigrants to towns, were feared less as potential revolutionaries than as the carriers and breeders of disease. Moreover, discrepancies of income were of an order that inhibited rather than encouraged class rivalry. In the neighbourhood of Valladolid the count of Benavente's annual income was seventeen hundred times that of a labourer; in the town itself, the income of a patrician of modest means was eighteen times that of a skilled craftsman and twenty-nine times that of an unskilled man. Social stratification, moreover, was broken up by clan affiliations, gilds, fraternities and clientage systems which restricted the ability to think in horizontal class terms and protectively associated men of low income with their betters.

Social tension in Europe was in any case far from uniform. At its most complex in countries with fairly dense populations, many towns, much commerce and well-established conventions defining the relations between government, corporation and individual—England, France, northern Italy, the Low Countries, central and southern Germany—it was also least disruptive there. In countries like Norway, Sweden and Spain, in which an urban middle class formed the thinnest of buffers between possessors and non-possessors, there was little occasion for tension within classes, and thinly dispersed populations, a vigilant church and a securely established customary law reduced the danger of tension between them. Moving eastward, however, beyond the limits of the Austrian Danube,

represented a breakdown in the ideal of service, of filling a useful place in society by devotedly serving a superior in return for his protection, an ideal that was not merely part of the nostalgia of chivalrous literature but still ensured harmony within the tradesman's house between master, apprentice and servant as well as within the complex social apparatus needed to run the vast households of the nobility. The ideal meant nothing—and never had—to men desperately on the make, it could wear thin in the relations of humanists to their patrons, and though it had risen within the military structure of feudalism it was openly denied now by professional soldiers who struck on the eve of battle for higher pay. However, it was from an understanding of the emotional satisfaction that service gave, as well as from its proved value as a social emollient, that the attacks on men's desire to change their station came.

In handbooks for merchants the emphasis was not on how to get ahead, how to make a fortune, but how to live up to the skills and virtues expected by society of a merchant. The same preoccupation with things as they were is shown in the many painted and engraved representations of the dress and occupations of different ranks, from emperor and money-changer to craftsman and beggar. They were shown for their own sake, or linked in a series like Manuel's in which death dances off with every man, whatever his position or trade, or, as in the engraved 'Tarocchi Cards', they were included with figures of the planets and virtues as part of a pre-ordained and unchangeable pattern of existence. Tableaux of occupations figured in public entertainments like the Schembart festival of Nuremberg, each distinguished by the costume which marked a man out in the street as a lawyer, a doctor, a shopkeeper or a smith. This visual cataloguing of class and occupation, like the increasing rigidity of craft organisation, the codification of laws and the working out of lists of precedence to determine who should enter when and sit where at diplomatic functions, reflects a tendency to see society as anything but open. The solemn state and religious processions in Venice were like animated diagrams of the three estates theory: doge and senators in one mass, the clergy in another, the separate crafts

tive of social divisions. To cite Erasmus again, whose works had a far wider distribution than those of any other intellectual: 'let others paint on their escutcheons lions, eagles, bulls, leopards. Those are the possessors of true nobility who can use on their coats of arms ideas which they have thoroughly learned from the liberal arts'; or, a propos unworthy nobleman, 'why, I ask you, should this class of person be placed on a higher level than the shoemaker or the farmer?' But this suggestion that nobility is essentially a property of the cultivated mind exerting itself in the interest of the common good was in earnest only at the level (a high one) of comment on the moral nature of man: transposed into actual social terms it was no more than a cosily *risqué* debating point. Castiglione raised it, only to head it smartly off. The unwelcome suggestion that the base-born can achieve rank was countered by the argument that good comes from good; the gentleman therefore would be careful not to besmirch his caste. The advice that followed was straightforward: the courtier should not wrestle with a peasant (it would damage his status if he lost); he should only dance with abandon among equals; he should mix sparingly with the people lest familiarity should breed contempt. Such advice shows how shakily realistic was the thesis that the good shoe-maker was more worthy of respect than the bad noble. Were not aristocrats (thus Edmund Dudley, in grotesque parody of Pico) inserted by God in His scheme of degrees between ordinary men and the angels?

Nor did those shavings from the block of humanist thought, Fortune and Opportunity, express an approach to social mobility. From paint to the cheapest woodcut, images were multiplied of Opportunity, the sprite-goddess with bald pate and waving forelock which the resourceful man could clutch before she dashed past him. In bronze and prose Fortune teetered on her globe or puffed the sails of her own ship, personified Whim, less deterministic than Fate, less mechanically efficient than the Wheel of Circumstance. Machiavelli, in a key chapter in his essay in the politically possible, *The Prince*, likened Fortune to a woman who could be shaken into submission. But if the message of these images was that man was

of tenure. Some offices were even, in effect, hereditary. It was a career that could not only lead to ennoblement but meant mingling with nobles both at court and in provincial centres on terms of mutual interest: satisfying in itself at a time when the aristocrat was the most widely revered social type, and for the opportunities this relationship gave for marrying into the noble class. Finally, thanks to the convention, commonest in France, whereby offices were actually sold for cash, it was possible for a merchant to buy his way in. It was a career in which few men climbed far, but because of their mixed social origin—noble, bourgeois, clerical—the nature of their occupation and the specific loyalty it encouraged, and because of the blend of respect and distrust with which they were regarded, the officials demand a place in the list of special classes to be considered before turning to the broader categories of country and town dwellers, and to the nobility.

The notion of the three estates was based on a view of society in which each estate aided the other two. The officials in the popular view, constituted a group which lived off, not for, the others. And with them were associated two other occupations, also seen as dedicated to self-interest at the expense of the rest of society: doctors and lawyers. Medicine was an academic subject in high repute—it was the best paid chair in most universities—but it was almost entirely a bookish subject, and shaded readily into astrology. Simon of Pavia, for instance, who doubled as physician and astrologer to Louis XI and Charles VIII, married into the aristocracy and died rich. Without a tradition of empirical research and increasingly dedicated to explaining the principles of classical medicine, doctors sought explanations in the stars rather than in the bloodstream, and preferred magical to clinical experiment. To retain the monetary advantage of being thought to be practical as well as learned, they were tempted to claim wondrous but secret cures and thus expose themselves to the charge of quackery. Wisely, the public relied mainly on herbs and traditional lore, invoking the physician only in moments of real desperation—moments when a case had usually gone far beyond the ability of medical science to cure it. The popular

blind and intricate laws'. And over and above their normal charges lawyers were universally accused of taking bribes. To have an appetite 'as indiscriminate as a lawyer's wallet' was already a proverbial expression in France. What is the most delicate thing in the world? A lawyer's shoulder: if you do but touch it his hand shoots out for money. In a multitude of expressions like this literature expressed society's distrust. Lawyers might be ministers of state, town clerks, bailiffs or manorial auditors, they were scattered up and down the ladder of incomes, but whatever their other functions, in whatever style they lived, they were seen, and saw themselves, primarily as men trained in the law, their numbers sustained by the litigiousness of the public and inflated by the need of bureaucracies for the nearest thing the age possessed to a higher technical education and an organised profession.

Proficiency in humanist studies could also lead to a career. To read and, still more, to write Latin with elegant fluency was a talent leading to such jobs as secretary to bishop or noble, historiographer to a ruler or a city, or to a chancery post which required adding the prestige of the fashionable Ciceronian style to official correspondence, proclamations, treaties and the formal allocutions with which diplomats presented their credentials. It was probably rare for a man to come to the law from a poor background, but many humanists had relatively humble origins—origins that could be concealed by the classless latinising of their names: Aesticampanus for Sommerfeld, for example or Laticephalus for Bredekopp. Celtis (born Bickel) was a peasant's son. Wimfeling's father was a saddler. Marineo Siculo was born to poor parents in the little Sicilian town of Vizzini. Illiterate until he was twenty-five, he learned to read from his nephew, his sister having married a little above her birth. He was then taken up by a kinsman priest and, by dint of fierce application, found a post as tutor in Palermo. From this shelter he achieved such a reputation that he went to a Chair in Salamanca in 1484 without having attended a university himself. The free-lance secular intellectuals were still a rare enough and a new enough phenomenon to be seen as a separate class, though as their talent was

some writers and painters with him 'and these are persons of
great importance and most dear to me'. Four years before that,
Lorenzo Costa, court painter to Francesco Gonzaga, duke of
Mantua, had flatly refused to paint the ducal children; Francesco's comment was a mild 'he has his quirks like most men
of genius'. In about 1512 Andrea del Sarto and *il Magnifico*
Giuliano de' Medici became fellow members of the convivial
Society of the Trowel in Florence. And (according to Vasari)
in 1506, when Michelangelo, who had walked out on a commission for Julius II, was shepherded back into his presence by
a bishop who begged the pope to excuse him because 'such
men as he were always ignorant', it was the bishop on whom
Julius's wrath fell for his outmoded view of an artist's personal qualities. This is all the more revealing for the fact that
Michelangelo's father, in whose veins was a faint trickle of
noble blood, had tried to beat the boy's determination to be
a sculptor out of him.

Apart from Michelangelo's frail gentility, the nobly-born
Gianfrancesco Rustici, and Leonardo's illegitimate begetting
by a prominent local notary, artists were predominantly of
commoner birth. Piero della Francesca's father was a cobbler,
Botticelli's a tanner, Fra Bartolommeo's a muleteer, Andrea del
Sarto's a tailor and Antonio and Piero Pollaiuolo's a poulterer.
And Lucas van Leyden, who married into the titled van
Boshuysen family, was one of the very few exceptions to the
rule that artists did not better themselves socially by marriage.
The gentleman-though-painter status was given willingly to
individuals whose works were in especial demand, but it left
no residuum after death or fall from favour. On the other hand,
the accumulation of information Vasari was able to collect
about this period for his *Lives* is itself an indication of the
interest taken in painters, sculptors and architects. He would
hardly have found the same harvest of facts if he had been
accumulating material for a history of the apothecaries. Nor, it
is fair to say, would he have found it outside Italy. In Robert
Wittinton's latin phrase book of 1520 'carvers, gravers, image-
makers and painters' were placed firmly between plasterers
and glaziers and thatchers and other 'labourers'.

the Parisian Jean Petit, who came from a family of master butchers, could set one up on his own. Alternatively a scholar could enlist support, as did Aldus that of Pico della Mirandola's family. Under these respectable social and financial auspices the best brains of the local community were enlisted to help with editing and proof-reading. When to this is added the collaboration of artists of the calibre of Dürer, Holbein, Burgkmair and the anonymous illustrator of the Venetian *Hypnerotomachia Polifili*, the attractiveness of the milieu to professional and dilettante scholars is easy to understand. Printers like Badius in Paris, Amorbach and Froben in Basel, Schürer in Cracow and Aldus in Venice ran institutions which, because of their continuity, their independence from the familiar centres of intellectual activity—universities and monasteries— and the social variety of their collaborators were far more influential in propagating the notion of an intelligentsia than were the temporary liaisons between painter, patron and scholarly adviser that characterised some of the great decorative cycles of the period.

Recognition of such a milieu had to some extent been prepared by the nature of the mid-fifteenth century scriptoria. The printing houses, however, generated a quite novel excitement. While conservatives could interpret the use of Greek fire to prove that the ancients had known about gunpowder, printing was incontrovertibly an invention of the moderns. And the possibility of mass-production occurred at a time when governments were keenly aware of the value of propaganda and when humanism had awakened a demand for critically edited texts which could not be met, either in volume or uniformity, by copyists. When to this we add the fact that an increasing number of local schools were turning out semi-literates with nothing to read, the spread of printing was assured. By the end of the fifteenth century the number of books printed has been estimated at six million, composed of about thirty thousand different titles produced by something like one thousand different printers. A professional copyist, working at pressure, took six months to cover four hundred folio leaves; it is not surprising that the printing offices were

of refining and smelting.

The miner could thus be an expert. Louis XI recruited miners from Germany and Ivan III imported German special-ists in 1491 to prospect for copper and silver along the river Pechora. Because of the value of his craft and the isolated but compact communities in which he worked, he was also a man accustomed to privileges. Miners were treated by governments with some caution, in Sweden they even sent delegates of their own to meetings of the estates. In time of war recruiting officers turned above all to the mining areas in their search for hardy, resourceful and quick-witted soldiers and pioneers.

In a similar way, the mercenary soldier represented an old trade given a new aspect by changing conditions. He thereby made a fresh impact on contemporary opinion and acquired a more formalised view of his own separateness from the rest of society. Wars were still fought by a majority of part-time soldiers, raised for a specific campaign and returning to their peacetime occupations at its conclusion, gentlemen and a few rich bourgeois on horseback, peasants and poorer townsmen on foot. The cost of maintaining an adequate standing army of professionals was too great to permit the breaking of this formula altogether, but its drawbacks were becoming increas-ingly clear. Peasants had always been reluctant to be long away from their crops, tradesmen from their shops. Though in most parts of Europe laymen between the ages of sixteen or thereabouts and sixty were required to keep weapons at home or in a local armoury, these were seldom, in spite of constant admonition, kept in good repair. And now, after the convinc-ing and widely publicised defeats of the Burgundian armies by the Swiss in the 1470s, two lessons had been learned. One was that heavy cavalry, the traditional noble arm, could not on their own defeat pikemen, and that armies now needed a more careful balance than any one country could easily muster—heavy and light horse, pikemen and halberdiers, archers and arquebusiers; the second was that a higher standard of train-ing was desirable than the part-time soldier was prepared to invest in against a crisis. For garrison duty, therefore, for permanent personal guards (like the Scots guard of the kings

needed to process others' products but who could set aside or
snip aside part of these products with little fear of detection.
Moral disapprobation was a second. Bath attendants' sons
were excluded from gilds because the public baths were commonly places of prostitution as well as the most convenient way
of getting clean. A third was unabsorption into legally constituted society: hence the German scorn for the linen-weavers,
who had no gild, no voice, therefore, in civic affairs, hence too
the distrust of wandering entertainers, however beguiling their
talents. The fourth was a latent hatred of those whose moral
standing was unknowable, who were not only without an
acknowledged place in the social hierarchy but were spiritually
alien as well. Most prominent in this category were the Jews.

By the late fifteenth century an uneasy compromise between
Jew and Christian had been worked out. It involved the yellow
badge (or its equivalent) and sudden and arbitrary taxation,
but it secured freedom of worship; the separateness was hardly
more galling than that of the localities into which communities of foreign Christian merchants might be herded, and
wealth could buy exemptions. Not only in trade and banking,
but as physicians, musicians and scholars the Jews made significant and welcomed contributions to some of the main-
streams of European life. An interest in Hebrew was growing*
but this interest in the language of Moses, of God's command-
ments to men and of Christ himself was the thinnest of ice
over the centuries-long prejudices of westernised Christianity.
Since the Vulgate bible of St. Jerome, God had spoken to
Europeans in Latin: Hebrew was the tongue of Judas, the be-
trayer. In painting after painting the Christ child blessed mankind among the ruins of the Old Law of the Hebrews, the
fractured arches of the stable symbolising the shift from Pales-
tine to Rome. Passion plays featured debates in which syna-
gogue was dialectically routed by church. When a new pope
moved in procession to St. Peters he was met on the bridge of
St. Angelo by the representatives of the Jewish community in

* See p. 301–2.

from sunset to sunrise, dates from 1516 when the Venetian Jews were sealed off in this way, the Jews by a natural exclusiveness had lived in a privacy which was an affront to the gregariousness of their neighbours, and a cause of suspicion: how was it that the Jews, who lived apart, almost, as it were, in secret, always seemed to have more money than the frank, open and loan-seeking Christian? Officially the church could accommodate itself to co-existence with the Jews as the church could co-exist with slavery, judicial torture, firearms, anything society appeared to need to keep it going, but individual clerics and, above all, public opinion found it difficult to accept the Jewish infection of the third estate. 'Why do the Jews not want to work with their hands?' asked the preacher Geiler of Kaysersberg. 'Are not they, as we are, subject to God's explicit commandment, "In the sweat of thy brow shalt thou eat bread"?' The Spanish chronicler Andres Bernaldez pointed out that the Jews 'never wanted to take jobs in ploughing or digging, nor would they go through the fields tending cattle, nor would they teach their children to do so; all their wish was a job in the town, and earning their living without much labour.'

In 1498 they were expelled from Nuremberg because (in this city based on the profit motive) of their 'evil, dangerous and cunning usurous dealings'. In the same year they were expelled from Würzburg, Salzburg and Württemberg, in 1499 from Ulm, in 1500 from Nördlingen, in each case with the permission (and to the financial advantage) of Maximilian. In France, expelled from certain towns (among them Tarascon, Saint-Maximin, Arles) they found refuge on papal territory at Avignon. In 1495, and again in 1506, they were banished from the whole of Provence; de Beatis commented that if the Jews went the few yards that separated papal from French jurisdiction 'anyone could put them fearlessly to death'. In 1502 Ivan III withdrew the measure of protection he had extended to Jews in Russia. But it was in Spain that social jealousy, religious euphoria, political calculation and, perhaps, population pressure produced the real catastrophe: in 1492 practising Jews were summarily expelled and

slave than an unregenerate freeman. The missionary orders did come to show—and it took considerable courage—a deep humanitarian concern for the lot of the indigenous populations of the Americas, but the importation of slaves from elsewhere had become too commonplace to prompt more than a flicker of concern about the institution of slavery itself.

The Portuguese had been importing African slaves for their own use well before they supplied them to the Spaniards for the mines and plantations of the New World. Some 150,000 had been shipped by 1500. Early in the sixteenth century an observer wrote, no doubt with some exaggeration, that 'one could almost believe that in Lisbon there are more slaves, male and female, than there are Portuguese of free condition.' In Italy, slaves had long been a familiar feature of wealthy households, and if their numbers were declining at the end of the century—though there may have been some 3,000 in Venice alone—this was not due to a change of attitude but to the blocking of a main source of supply by Turkish control of the Black Sea and Levantine ports. Henceforward the Turks absorbed the multi-racial products of the Kaffa market, and Italian, Spanish and Portuguese merchants were left with Ethiopians, Moors from the north African littoral and a few Greeks and Slavs picked up in Dalmatia. Black slaves were, besides, becoming more expensive, and in bourgeois households had proved a tiresome moral problem: their chattel-like availability enabling their owners to test an already well-developed lore about the potency of the African. They were now bought principally as pets, welcome as a note of dusky exoticism in the fashionable *ensemble* of a court. Ippolito de Medici's negro wrestlers, the one hundred Moors, a present from Ferdinand to Innocent VIII in 1488, whom the pope distributed among his cardinals and the Roman nobles he wished to favour, had a productive value of zero. This is probably true of south-western Europe as a whole (slavery had long disappeared in the north-west) by 1500. The Mediterranean galley-slave is a phenomenon of the mid-sixteenth century. Though ship's captains used captured natives overseas, on voyages from Europe the men chosen for pump duty

most were employed as servants or bodyguards. For boys from
the age of twelve or so, either bought in slave markets or recruited as part of the human tribute levied by the Turks
among the Albanians, Serbians, Croatians, Bulgarians and
Greeks, the possibility of social mobility—apart from legal
status—was enormously greater than in the west, a factor
which caused many Balkan parents to welcome the four-yearly
posse of child inspectors, and even prompted Muslim families
to pay Christians to pass off their children as their own. The
administrative and military services of the Ottoman state, were
recruited from re-educated young Christian slaves, and a
career started in an Albanian hovel could lead to a generalship,
a capacious harem and a household running into thousands.
The lot of the tribute children was in dramatic contrast to that
of the negro plantation worker in Hispaniola or of those still
less fortunate Guineans sold by the French to their cannibal
associates in Brazil, the Potiguara, as food.

### iii

From government officials and painters to miners and slaves
we have been dealing with anomalies within the third estate.
Work was overwhelmingly a matter of tilling the soil, and the
population of Europe was overwhelmingly a population of
peasants. In 1510 Lucas van Leyden commemorated this fact
in a moving engraving of Adam and Eve. The two figures
walk across a landscape of stones and coarse grass, backed by
a tree pollarded by gales. Eve, as the prefiguration of Mary
(Quos Evae culpa damnavit, Mariae gratia solvit) and the
symbol of all motherhood, fits into this toilsome background
but is not of it; with brooding face and flying hair, her body
and dress a marvellous blend of gothic with the antique, she
cradles a child who sits in her arms like a plump baby abbot.
Timeless and classless, mother and child are escorted across
the picture by a figure that seems to have grown out of the
landscape and is doomed to stay in it; an old man, with wild
beard and hair, his neck stooping from enormous shoulders,

take account. With no privacy—the majority had one or two-roomed hovels which doubled as barn and stable—and few possessions, a table, a chest (for storage and to sit on), an iron pot and a kneading trough, with children who were set to scare birds as soon as they could toddle and a wife who worked as hard as he, the peasant was unfitted to become involved with changes in the superstructure of the civilisation of which he was the foundation. The voice with which he speaks from the written sources is violent, litigious, full of crude superstition. But this is because we hear him most clearly when he is up against government or being denounced from the pulpit. His endurance, his ability to work with others, his urge to collect land and stock of his own: these can best be seen in the land itself and the marks of his work in it, and for the rest we must turn to the peasants of modern Europe, of, for example, Montenegro or Sardinia or Ireland, to see how an ignorant conservatism can include generosity and humour.

A quick survey of Europe from west to east will show the regional variations against which these generalisations must be measured and how wide was the contrast between the reasonably prosperous peasantry of England and France and the declining status and living standards in Poland and Russia.

The variety in England was especially great. A gradually rising population meant that men with little or no land of their own, who relied on being employed by others, were meeting greater competition and being forced into reliance on charity. The same factor brought insecurity into the lives of the large number of cottagers, men who owned a house and a few acres of land but who looked to seasonal work for others to keep their families safely over the subsistence level. On the other hand, during the labour shortage after the Black Death significant numbers of peasants had bought or bargained their way into small farms of their own (or, if not absolutely their own in law, capable of being handed on without question to their heirs). The result was to increase the gap between the landless man and cottager and the smallholder who, while still working himself on the land, employed shepherds and labourers. Such a man might look forward to the time when

If the wealth of published material relating to English and French rural life makes generalisation hazardous, any conclusions about the position of the Spanish peasantry are temerarious for the opposite reason. A decree of the *cortes* held at Toledo in 1480 abolished servile tenure in Castile and feudal services were abolished for Catalonia in 1486 in return for a cash compensation. How far the peasantry actually benefited from these measures, in contrast to Aragon, where feudal relationships remained in force, it is impossible to say. There were enough prosperous peasant proprietors in Castile to be recognised as a social type in literature, but the possibility of a poor man's improving his status was severely inhibited by the massive support given by the government to the pasturage routes for the giant sheep flocks organised by the *Mesta*. In the peninsula as a whole it was further inhibited by the weight of seigneurial dues, state taxes and church tithes; for most peasants a life of desperate toil left their fortunes exactly as they had inherited them and provided no insurance against the indebtedness that followed a bad harvest. In Portugal rent, feudal dues and tithe could account for seventy per cent of a peasant's produce.

Yet this was not, in Spain or Portugal, a time when peasant revolt, let alone peasant war was feared. King John of Denmark (1481–1513) could safely refer to the peasants as men born to servitude (a condition into which, in contrast to Sweden, they were declining in his reign). The French proverb 'Jaques Bonhomme has a strong back and will bear anything' took the peasant's passivity for granted, as did the German 'a peasant is just like an ox, only he has no horns'— though peasant wars were to break out in southern and central Germany in 1524–25 and were preceded by clandestine associations like the *Bundschuh* movement of 1502–1517. For its size and the heterogeneity of its institutions, Germany was, of all European countries, the one about which it is most dangerous to generalise, but the status and prosperity of the peasant (and therefore the range between poor and well-to-do) seems to have been highest in the south-west and to have dwindled towards the north-east. Speaking of Alsace, Wim-

landowners. In 1497 the Bohemian diet affirmed the servitude of peasants. In 1519 the service due for a peasant holding was declared by statute to be one day a week (in lieu of from one to six days a year) and was in practice considerably heavier; by a series of laws passed from 1496 to 1511 neither a peasant nor his sons could leave the land without his master's consent, and during the same period right of appeal from seigneurial justice was removed from all but church and crown lands. In 1514 all Hungarian peasants outside the royal free boroughs were condemned to 'real and perpetual servitude' to their masters. The same debasement in status and freedom of action proceeded in Lithuania and Russia, with increased demands both for money dues and labour services and with a firmer tying of the peasant to the soil; by the Russian Code of 1497 a peasant could only leave his lord during the two weeks following St. George's day and only then after paying heavy fees for the privilege of being a free man for one twenty-sixth of the year.

A prime cause of this descent into serfdom was the declining importance of towns and of influential urban classes in eastern Europe. Noble resentment of the rival marketing activities of the towns, the high prices charged there for manufactured goods, the refuge they gave to runaway peasants and the consideration given them by rulers in need of cash subsidies; these factors led to a successful pressure on governments to reduce the independence and the commercial activity of the towns. And this pressure came at a time when the Hanseatic League, itself in decline and harassed in the Baltic by English and Dutch shipping, could no longer act as an example of urban energy in north eastern Europe, and when the westward overland trade routes virtually dried up when the Turks occupied the north coast of the Black Sea. In 1500 townsmen were excluded from representation in the Bohemian diet; they regained it in 1517, but the tendency was clear: nobles, with the support of government, confronted the peasants without the political and economic buffer of the towns.

This is not to say that bourgeois activity ceased in the east:

impressively seen to constitute an estate of their own and the connection of some of the great merchant families with the royal administration gave an extra publicity to their status. Above all, perhaps, the increasing range of incomes and styles of living among the bourgeoisie as a whole caught the attention of contemporaries more vividly than before.

How wide the range of incomes among the bourgeoisie could be by 1500, may be seen from a reasonably thriving, middling large town, Hamburg, in which four categories have been distinguished:* the rich, with incomes varying from 5,000 to 40,000 Lübeck marks—the great merchants and property owners; those with incomes between 2,000 and 5,000 marks, mostly men engaged in brewing or shipping; the smaller brewers, prosperous shopkeepers, notably butchers and goldsmiths, with between 600 and 2,000 marks; lesser tradesmen and the numerous brewers who rented, rather than owned their premises—150 to 600 marks. Below these categories came the mass of poor artisans, municipal employees, such as street cleaners, porters and domestic servants.

Taken in conjunction with comparable studies at different times, such figures tend to show that there was a fairly general tendency in European towns for the contrasts both between rich and poor bourgeois and between the bourgeoisie as a whole and manual workers to become more marked. A case in point is Nuremberg, which shared the rise in production characteristic of many German cities between 1480 and 1520. The discrepancy here between the poor and the very rich has been described as 'enormous'† but no easy correlation can be made between wealth, status and political power. Political control was firmly in the hands of forty-three patrician families, themselves divided into three categories according to the antiquity of their association with civic administration. Formally closing admission into the ranks of the patriciate in 1521, the Council defined this class as 'those families who used to

* By Heinrich Reincke, quo. P. Dollinger, *La Hanse* (paris, 1964) 165.

† By Gerald Strauss in his *Nuremberg in the Sixteenth Century* (N.Y. 1966) from which I take the following details.

that 'on la demoisellera'. Conquillart suggests that, meanwhile, she should be dressed half in linen and half in velvet,
'moytie bourgeoise et demoyselle'.

It was in fact probably more common for rich bourgeois to
pass upwards into the ranks of the aristocracy, by acceptance
if not by patent of nobility, than for a poor man to prosper his
way into those levels of the bourgeoisie where the real social
weight lay. Urban society was ancient. The distribution of
power in municipal affairs had long been stabilised among the
representatives of various trades or crafts and little allowance
had been made for the economic changes of the past century
or so. Because recruitment into the mastership ranks of the
gilds was becoming increasingly restricted, the industrious
apprentice who makes good was too rare to be, as yet, a
symbol of social success. While a master could take his own
sons as apprentices without restriction, one or two outsiders
was usually the limit, and then, after an apprenticeship of
from four to eight years, the qualified journeyman had to find
work for himself until he could accumulate the fee which
could purchase him a mastership of his own.

The tendency for the mastership class to become self-
perpetuating, and for status to be determined by tradition and
family rather than talent or response to market fluctuations,
hardened at a time when immigration into the towns was increasing and when rising prices forced the salaried journeyman and the urban labourer either to a restless itinerancy or
to a nearness to the bread-line that caused a further harden-
ing of the ranks above them; the existence of a hard-pressed
proletariat was not a novel, but became a more noticeable
phenomenon. 'In all', it has been said of England, 'up to two-
thirds of the urban population lived near or below the poverty
line; the top third constituted a social pyramid rising to a
needle-like point—through prosperous artificers, tradesmen
and professional men to the single merchant who might alone
pay up to a third of the subsidy due from the community.'*

Desperate men, however, had neither the energy, nor the

* Joan Simon, *Education and Society in Tudor England* (Cambridge, 1966) 18.

monly the prerogative of the younger sons of noble families. Especially in Germany, nobles dominated the cathedral chapters. Erasmus, informed that entry to the Strasburg chapter was open only to those who could muster twelve aristocratic forbears on both the father's and mother's side, commented that 'Christ himself could not have entered this college without a dispensation.' But for every magnate who lorded it over great demesnes fattened by shrewd marriage alliances and defended by the prestige of ecclesiastic relatives, there were many aristocrats who only just managed, snarling and miserable, to hang on to their increasingly anachronistic rôle. Writing to Willibald Pirckheimer, von Hutten described his life as a free knight of the Empire. 'Do not envy me my life as compared with yours ... We live in fields, forests and fortresses. Those by whose labours we exist are poverty-stricken peasants, to whom we lease our fields, vineyards, pastures and woods. The return is exceedingly sparse in proportion to the labour expended ... I must attach myself to some prince in the hope of protection. Otherwise everyone will look upon me as fair plunder ... We cannot visit a neighbouring village or go hunting and fishing save in iron ... The castle, whether on plain or mountain, must be not fair but firm, surrounded by moat and wall, narrow within, crowded with stalls for the cattle and arsenals for guns, pitch and powder. Then there are dogs and their dung, a sweet savour, I assure you. The horsemen come and go, among them robbers, thieves and bandits ... The day is full of thought for the morrow, constant disturbance, continual storms ... If the harvest fails in any year, then follow dire poverty, unrest and turbulence.'*

Within the aristocratic caste there were, indeed, clear gradations of dignity—in England from duke and marquis through baron and knight to esquire and gentleman—and one reasonably clear distinction of class: between the prepotent aristocrats and the men of heraldically recognised descent but moderate standing, a class identified with the gentry in England, the *petite noblesse* in France, the Polish *szlachta*, the

---

* Hajo Holborn, *Ulrich von Hutten and the German Reformation* (N.Y. 1966) 18–19.

the caste frontier into legal studies and, more rarely, into commerce.

The shrinking of political independence and a weakening economic position did not have a profound social effect. Among the nobility the transition from quasi-prince to grandee is easier to detect now than it was then. In some countries— France, Spain and Hungary among them—aristocrats were exempt from taxation; in all they were taxed separately, and their distinction from the bourgeoisie was thus still seen in high relief. New creations from bourgeois blood were numerous, but not so frequent as to maim the prestige of aristocratic birth. And an aura of social distance was enhanced by a revival of chivalric manners. Malory's *Morte D'Arthur*, printed in 1485 by Caxton and in 1498 by Wynkyn de Worde, suggested that 'all gentlemen that bear old arms ought of right to honour Sir Tristram for the goodly terms that gentlemen have and use . . . that thereby . . . all men of worship may dissever [distinguish] a gentleman from a yeoman.' The late fifteenth century Gothic revival of manners followed the spirit of this advice. The tournament was revived with full medieval ceremony and a new heraldic sophistication. It was sharply restricted to gentlemen; in England no one lower than the rank of esquire could compete, in Germany, to keep out the recently ennobled, the number of noble forbears necessary to qualify was increased to eight, even at times to sixteen. And alongside the freshened cult of the tournament there was a wave of legislation to restore to the knightly class their neglected hunting rights both over the 'greater hunting' of deer, wild boar, bears and wolves and the 'lesser hunting' of wildfowl and hares.

It was a revival that both reassured the aristocrat that he was different in kind from other men and heightened the attractiveness of the aristocratic milieu to the bourgeois. For the neo-chivalry of this period was a fashion and fashion was something the bourgeois understood. Indeed, in some places he set it. 'Extravagance in dress has impoverished the German nobility', a German moralist wrote sadly. 'They desire to make the same show as the rich city merchants. Heretofore they

to the notion of service to the community, showed signs of envying the individualism, or, rather, the comparative irresponsibility of the seigneur. Nor did he have to look across the Alps to see the seigneur raising troops, exercising personal justice or setting his bravos on officers of the state: in Milan and Naples the late fifteenth century saw a growing use of military tenures and feudal relationships.

Italian respect for the way of life of the invading aristocracies was not based on respect for their intellectual attainments. Castiglione expressed the hope that were the cultivated duke of Angoulême to succeed Louis XII (as he did) the French might at last acquire a culture that would begin to match their valour. Sebastian Franck wrote of German aristocrats that 'they have no occupation but hunting with dog and falcon, guzzling and carousing.' But no blanket condemnation of this sort is really revealing. German aristocrats' sons, for instance, went in impressive numbers to universities.

In the same way, the English aristocracy were probably literate in the main in spite of the humanist Richard Pace's famous anecdote about the outburst of an English squire: 'I swear by God's body I'd rather that my son should hang than study letters. For it becomes the sons of gentlemen to blow the horn knowledgeably, to hunt skilfully, and elegantly carry and train a hawk. But the study of letters should be left to the sons of rustics.' Changing conditions were showing that prestige and economic advancement called for hornbook as well as horn. Educated princes were seeking educated advisers and public servants, and were increasingly finding them among the bourgeoisie. That contemporaries recognised this is witnessed by a nervous spurt of anti-bourgeois satire sponsored by noble patrons. And that satire was not enough is shown in Edmund Dudley's warning 'verily I fear me the noblemen and gentlemen of England be the worst brought up for the most part of any realm of Christendom. And therefore the children of poor men and mean folk are promoted to the authority that the children of noble blood should have if they were meet therefore.'

bears striking witness to the extent to which Europeans were conditioned to see, as well as to think, in terms of Christianity. Centuries of crusading, trade and pilgrimages had done little to open Christian eyes to the nature of Mohammedanism, Christianity's neighbour and rival faith. There was as little attempt to understand the true nature of a faith practised in Europe itself: that of the Jews. When the Cabala was studied, by Pico della Mirandola and Reuchlin, it was as part of the literary archaeology of Christianity. The study of Hebrew was, indeed, undertaken seriously. Reuchlin's grammar was published in 1506 and the language was taught at several universities, among them Alcala, Louvain, Wittenberg and Oxford. But this was in the interest of studying the Old Testament, not Judaism. It was not a time of challenging heresies within Christendom itself. Relations between Catholics and Orthodox were on the whole calm; in Corfu Romans and Greeks shared in religious processions and once a year the church of St. Arsenios was discordant with their two styles of chanting. But the great debates, the efforts to reach formal reconciliation through mutual understanding, had ceased since the mid-century. To see a Hindu temple in terms of a Christian church was an extreme case, but it is not surprising that other explorers should show little interest in the beliefs of the peoples they came upon. 'They have no faith,' wrote Alvise Cadamosto of the inhabitants of the Canary Islands. 'They do not have or understand any belief' was Caminha's comment on the natives of Brazil. Spiritually, the non-European peoples were seen as *tabulae rasae* on which the elements of Christianity had merely to be scratched. Or when (as with the Aztecs) a flourishing priesthood drew attention to a systematised faith, it was above all the similarities to Christian practice that were commented on. It was not until widespread backsliding from superficial conversions became an outstanding missionary problem that Christians realised that it was necessary to study and to understand rival faiths in order to attack them at the roots, a development that coincided with the Reformation's redirection of interest to faith rather than morals.

statute of 1513 put this identity of interest very clearly. 'For-
asmuch as it is often seen that man's reason, whereby he
should discern the good from the evil and the right from
wrong is many times, by seduction of the Devil . . . repressed
and vanquished, whereupon commonly ensues discords, mur-
ders, robberies, divisions, disobeisance to sovereigns, sub-
version of realms and destruction of peoples, . . . therefore emperors, princes and governors of time past, for refraining of
such inordinate appetites and punishment of those folks which
rather eschew to offend for fear of bodily pain or losses of
goods than for the love of God or justice, full wisely and
politicly ordained divers laws serving to the same purpose as
well in time of war as peace.' Cabral, following up da Gama's
voyage, carried with him a letter to the ruler of Calicut warning him that now God had pointed out a way by which Europeans could dominate the trade of his country he should not
wish to resist His manifest and known will. Machiavelli's
'crime' was not that by detaching political planning from the
background of Christian morality he invited rulers to be
wicked: by that criterion they were wicked anyway, but that
he deprived actions of state from carrying with them the
savour of divine approval.

Between the church's insinuation of its control into the
privacies of domestic life and the suggestion that to break
the law was to disobey God, a third aspect of secular-clerical
relations affected the way in which men thought about religion: the connection between the church in a particular
country and the papacy. Notionally, Christendom was one.
When popes called for a crusade, individual states had at least
to expend some effort of ingenuity in explaining why they
could not contribute to it. Notionally, popes were supreme
diplomatic arbiters. 'It is the proper function of the Roman pon-
tiff, of the cardinals, of bishops and abbots', Erasmus wrote in
1514, 'to compose the quarrels of Christian princes, to exert
their authority in this field and show how far the reverence of
their office prevails.' Papal assistance was indeed invoked to
bring about an agreement between the Swiss and Milan in
1483, and to confirm the Anglo-French treaty of 1498. Leo

pressed) the spiritual as well as the secular head. Anti-papal feeling, however, though stronger in Germany than elsewhere, was impossible to mobilise among the competing interests of the Empire and remained in a state of baffled suspense, eased here and there by local 'concordats' granted to individual princes, and ventilated in meetings of the imperial diet as 'the grievances of the German nation'—complaints about the fiscal and jurisdictional greed of the papacy and the need for the moral reform of the clergy. Maximilian's cloudy Caesaro-papism was echoed more purposefully in Russia when Ivan III took advantage of the notion that now Rome (in Orthodox eyes) was heretical and Constantinople conquered, Moscow was the Third Rome, the true centre of Christianity. Ivan drew liberally on the image and on the ceremony of Byzantium. He promoted the idea of his protectorship of the church and pushed steadily for a real control over it, a tendency supported by churchmen themselves partly as a lesser evil than control by local nobles, and partly because an influential minority believed that ecclesiastics should not possess material wealth. The secularisation of the possessions of churches and monasteries after the capture of Novgorod provided a model for a cautious policy of secularisation in the grand duchy of Moscow, and the Third Rome theory a respectable cover for this aim. For as abbot Filotheus (Filofei) wrote to Ivan's son in 1510, 'he [Ivan] is on earth the sole emperor of the Christians, the leader of the Apostolic Church which stands no longer in Rome or in Constantinople, but in the blessed city of Moscow. She alone shines in the whole world brighter than the sun.' In no other European country did the church see its mission as so intimately linked to the authority of the ruler.

The church in France had a clear image of itself as inheriting rights and liberties, summed up in the word Gallicanism, that gave it considerable independence from Rome and assumed a corresponding subservience to the crown. The monarch was termed 'Most Christian'. The holy *ampoule* containing the chrism with which he was annointed at his coronation, entitled him to work miracles, curing sufferers from

tinued. The king did agree to certain principles governing nominations: candidates for bishoprics should be at least twenty-seven years old, for priorships and abbacies at least twenty-three, prospective bishops should have graduated in theology—there were other safeguards, but there were also enough exceptions (members of the royal household, '*personnes sublimes*') to preserve something of the old, energy-consuming uncertainty. In sum, the churchmen in France looked less to the papacy and more—and in an increasingly place-seeking mood—to the crown. The sufferers from this narrowing church-state relationship were the population at large and the lower ranks of the clergy. The eldest daughter of the church was becoming the fine lady she remained until the Revolution of 1789.

In no case, however, it is easy to judge the effect of church–state relations, either internally or between a nation and the papacy, on the quality of religious life among the people at large. The nature of the clergy, the respect in which they were held, the effectiveness of their ministry, these were directly related to the way in which they were appointed. But while a pope might impose an unpopular foreigner, a king might appoint a favourite with no religious qualifications. Anticlericalism, omnipresent, and ranging all the way from pastime to passion, almost certainly affected the quality of men's spiritual involvement in their religious practice, and one element in it was the question of church property. Yet it was as rabid in Scotland and northern Italy, where land had been steadily passing out of the control of the church into the hands of laymen, as it was in Germany, where ecclesiastical estates were still of formidable proportions.

ii

The closer the links between church and state, the more natural it seemed to look on the life of religion as a career, in which, by stepping sideways from the aristocracy or the bourgeoisie to the adjacent niche in the ecclesiastical hierachy, a

Scandal, of course, leaps to the eye, both for its own sake, and because it fascinated contemporaries. To supplement chronicles with diocesan records is to reveal bishops, possibly a majority, who ran their sees with an eye to their pastoral responsibilities. In England, lack of contact between bishops and the life of the parish was probably due as much to the great size of the dioceses as to their secular preoccupations or to pluralism, and possibly this is true of Castile, where Isabella sought to fill vacant bishoprics with men of proved devotion. An Albert of Brandenburg, however, was responsible for a thousand times the number of souls in the care of a 'good' bishop like Fisher of Rochester or François d'Estaing of Rodez. And absences on secular business, frequent migration from benefice to benefice meant that many sees were without effective leadership, governed by deputies who either sought to imitate their superiors or were forced to devote themselves to routine administration rather than actively supervising the priests who were primarily responsible for sustaining the faith of the people. The church was coming to resemble a business which, secure from competition, ploughs its profits into directors' salaries and leaves its sales force slack or despairing. All the same, consistency of behaviour as a badge of deep religious feeling was not then taken for granted. A peasant's faith did not die because he saw his bishop's face in a sweat from hunting any more than a journeyman thought a cathedral was less the house of God because he came to sell his labour there.

The same caution must be borne in mind when considering Rome itself and the influence on the tone of religion in Europe of the reputation of the remarkable popes of this period, notably Alexander VI, Julius II and Leo X, together with their hardly less remarkable entourage of cardinals. Alexander's election was unfairly believed to be the result of bribery during the conclave, and his unpopularity as a Spaniard and his unconcealed regard for his children led to a proliferation of scandalous stories. 'There is no sort of outrage or vice', declared an anonymous pamphlet in 1501, 'that is not openly practised in the palace of the pope ... Rodrigo Borgia is an

be proved, popes were criticised for excessive pomp, political militancy, manipulation of the college of cardinals, the sale of offices, and nepotism. The triple nature of the papacy (its spiritual leadership, its sovereign role in a political entity, the States of the Church, and its governorship of a financial empire) was thrown into high relief in this period by the almost constant threat of diplomatic pressure or actual war. As territorial princes the popes were weak: areas formerly belonging to their States had been annexed by others (Bologna and Urbino were two cases); they had not solved the problem of assimilating the local feudal baronage. They needed money (which the succession of concordats had reduced) to raise armies and play the diplomatic game from a position of strength. They needed loyal lieutenants, and popes, who apart from Leo, were old men when they were elected and who could leave no dynasty behind them, found it harder to secure them than did other princes. They strained the conventions, then, selling offices to garner cash, and they used members of their families, whom they could trust. Like their fellow princes who were insisting on a greater measure of positive political control, the popes, by inflating the college of cardinals with their nominees and by-passing traditional chains of command, were putting themselves in a position to take quick decisions and have them acted upon. The need to behave like other territorial rulers, and their growing ability to do so, threw the secular aspects of the papal role into high relief. Even so, the multiple role was familiar to influential visitors, diplomats and churchmen, from the similar roles played by leading clerics in their own countries. Popes were criticised for particular policies, seldom for acting as politicians. Hearing of the death of Alexander VI in 1503, a Florentine merchant passed on the news to an associate abroad with no reference to Alexander's moral or spiritual qualities, or those to be hoped for in his successor. He simply prayed that 'with the help of God' a pope would be elected capable of keeping order in the Romagna, for 'business in all regions in this section is in such a state that it must be stimulated.'

It was, besides, less the popes than the bearing of the

Europe, in fact, order combatted order (on occasion scuffling for first place in processions) and parish clergy bewailed the 'poaching' activities of the friars, who, it was claimed, undermined pastoral discipline by granting easier penances and who even admitted the excommunicated to their services. When to this variety of complaints within the ranks of the church itself is added the complaints of the laity, a sorry picture emerges, even allowing for the fact that jokes and moans at the expense of monk and friar had such a venerable ancestry that they had lost much of their cutting edge.

The condition revealed by visitations and reform commissions was indeed deplorable; lax discipline, the neglect of vows, concubinage, ignorance, domestic squabbles. The accounts are most telling, perhaps, when they are least sensational, when they describe not the potations of wealthy abbots, or those Andalusian friars who chose—four hundred of them —to emigrate to Africa and embrace Islam rather than give up the embraces of their concubines, but isolated communities that had gone back, as it were, to the bush, coping with hardships and enjoying the rough pleasures of the ordinary rural hamlet, distinguishable from a settlement of peasants by little more than their dress, and not always by that; or those wealthier foundations, filled with the offspring of poor noble families, few in priest's orders, who with their hunting and hawking and brawling made their abbeys seem like baronial castles *en masquerade*. The causes of this decay were obvious enough. Men and women were admitted too easily and not instructed properly once they had entered; peasants sent their children for reasons of prestige, aristocrats treated monasteries and abbeys as privileged systems of relief from a too numerous brood. Yet in many monasteries the numbers had so dropped that almost every monk was needed to fill some office and it was impossible to discipline them by demotion. In others an abbot had been put in by force over the heads of the community and was treated with sullen resentment. The absenteeism of superiors, inadequate or intermittent inspection: there are explanations to be found in the structure of monasticism as a whole as well as in the quality of individuals. Challenged on

parishioners recognised that their efficacy depended on the nature of the priesthood and doubtful how many priests would have been capable of explaining it to them. Baptism, confession, marriage, extreme unction: the practice of religion was deeply engrained as a social habit; the comfort brought by the sacraments was, for a largely illiterate population, independent of theological understanding. The lower clergy were theologically naive because it was becoming harder for really poor children to get into universities, whose bursaries, primarily intended for the poor, were taken up by the children of the bourgeoisie. For reasons of poverty, large numbers completed only a part of their university course while many more got no further than the four year arts course which included no theology. Admission to the priesthood itself was perfunctory and unsearching and produced a mass of unpromotable clerics whose influence on their congregations depended on the accident of personal integrity unsupported by reasoned belief. Criticism and exhortation from above could do little. A reforming provincial of a monastic order at least had groups of men to deal with; a reforming bishop was hampered by the scattered nature of his charge. And his poverty made it almost impossible for a parish priest to better himself. His tithes had commonly been subjected to so many legal and landholding charges in the past centuries that he was left with but a fraction of them. A tax could reduce him to real misery. He depended, then, on fees. 'One year', ran an Italian anecdote of the time, 'the harvest of grain and fruit was excellent all over Italy and Tuscany, especially in the countryside around Florence. Everybody was rejoicing and talking about the large harvest of his land. One day priest Arlotto was with a group of men who were talking about their good luck; and after he had listened to them for a while, he said: "I had a completely different experience from yours; I can assure you that my best plot of land gave me a very poor crop." All the men who were in Arlotto's company were amazed and asked him how that could be possible, and what plot he was talking about that had produced such a poor crop. "It is the cemetery behind my church," he replied, "every year it gives me an

heretofore and less exclusive, was still active, a source of inspiration to those who in growing numbers clustered in the
great centres of theology, among which the university of
Paris remained pre-eminent, and penetrating downwards
through printed books and the spoken word of the pulpit.
There was no dominating figure; men looked back, and fruit-
fully, to the great seminal thinkers, Augustine, William of
Occam and Aquinas. Scholasticism, the mode of study and
expression characteristic of the faculties of theology, was under
attack, but the attack was violent because of the vitality, not
the flabbiness of what it was assaulting. The pastoral influence
of theological controversies had always been scant: that had
been the work of movements which, like the Franciscan, had
started at the pastoral level and then influenced theological
scholarship. Intricate and argumentative rather than morally
passionate, insulated from the church at large, theology remained vigorous and controversial. The danger was not that
the church had lost its reservoir of learning, its ability to train
and stimulate, but that too many of its leaders were appointed
to their positions without coming into prolonged or, indeed,
any contact with it.

The church's attitude to secular latin literature was mixed.
While Leo X was watching Terentian comedies in Rome, Guillaume Michel was continuing the medieval tradition of a
christianised Ovid with his edition of Virgil's *Georgics*, 'trans-
lated [into French] and moralised'. Virgil had referred to a
swarm of legless bees hatched in the body of a calf, a straightforward, if unusual, piece of rural observation; Michel was
quick to compare them with 'the new man regenerated in the
blood of Jesus Christ, with no power of his own to walk and
make progress along the path of virtue.' While in Italy the
followers of Pico della Mirandola were attempting to break
the divine code concealed in pre-Christian classical literature,
the abbess of the convent of St. Clara wrote to Konrad Celtis
thanking him for sending her his description of Nuremberg
and a copy of latin love poems, his *Amores*. 'I cannot in truth
deny that the description and praise of the earthly fatherland
in your book, which pleased me very much, would be even

The number of religious books is all the more revealing when it is born in mind that the introduction of printing enabled a country's whole manuscript literature, from cookery books and chivalrous romances to chronicles and poems—works accumulating over centuries—to get into circulation for the first time at a reasonable price. The queue, as it were, was jammed, and yet among new books popular demand gave pride of place to books on religious themes.

The effect on men's religious attitudes is impossible to gauge. Of heretical works there was hardly a sign before the spread of Lutheran books began. Sebastian Brant, it is true, complained that

> *Creeds, dogmas false in every way*
> *Now seem to grow from day to day.*
> *The printers make the case more dire:*
> *If some books went into the fire*
> *Much wrong and error would be gone.*

But it is doubtful if he had in mind more than the pullulation of accounts of false miracles and trite interpretations of scripture that degraded but did not challenge orthodox belief. On the other hand, works were published which, while not criticising the church, enabled men to define the nature of their dissatisfaction with it. Before 1501 the Bible had appeared in over ninety Latin and, in six languages, thirty vernacular editions. One of the works most frequently reprinted was the *Imitation of Christ*, again in vernacular translations as well as in Latin. Only a small proportion of the population was literate and the distribution of such books, even assuming an edition of one thousand copies each and a readership of five for each copy, affected only a fraction of that population. Against this, inventories in wills suggest that even reasonably well-to-do families possessed very few books, probably most had only one or two, and one book, read and re-read, prized and protected, tends to become The Book. The church had always been suspicious of the unsupervised reading of the Bible, especially of the Gospels: a contrast between the manners of Galilee and

to all levels of intellectual sophistication, were masters of both anecdote and argument, could terrify, inspire and charm.

As with books, it is extremely difficult to gauge the effect of sermons. Many, certainly, were violently emotional. The apothecary Luca Landucci, a devoted follower of Savonarola, noted in his diary that when the friar began to preach again in defiance of Alexander VI's prohibition, 'many people went there, and it was much talked of on account of his excommunication; and many did not go, for fear of being excommunicated, saying: *guista vel inguista, timenda est*'. And he added, 'I was one of those who did not go.' If any moral can be drawn from the confrontation between Savonarola, the preacher we know best, and Landucci, one of the very few assiduous attenders of sermons who has left any trace of his reactions, it is that even at a time of political and millenarian tension neither faith nor psychological equilibrium was easy to shake. Again, it has been suggested that the *contemptus mundi* emphasis created an atmosphere of despairing alarm, that the constant attacks on the avarice of merchants, the luxury of the nobles and their indifference to those in need encouraged class antagonism. It is doubtful. These themes were centuries old. When attempts to control preaching were made, as by the Lateran Council of 1516, it was heresy and inflammatory prophecies that came under scrutiny, not attacks on the rich or on the great, not even on the clergy themselves; indeed, it is more likely that support for the church was undermined by the continual washing of its own dirty linen in the pulpit.

Religion had a dark side of anguish and morbidity but this was at least as much the result of fear, physical fear in the face of plague, dearth and violence, as of the soul which feels itself doomed never to be illuminated by the presence of God, to be fouled eternally by sin. The church was careful to leave escape routes for the sinful: the mediation of the priesthood, the warnings of the confessional, the possibility of good works. Unless there was suspicion of downright heresy, its yoke was laid fairly lightly on the conscience of the individual. The penances imposed by the church courts for offences like adul-

ginnings in the 1470s, and that the stations of the cross became a familiar worship though, as the stations had not yet
been fixed along the Via Dolorosa itself in Jerusalem, the
ritual varied between one church and another. Nor was this
flexibility shown only towards popular aspirations. Growing
emphasis on the dignity of man among humanist scholars led
to an insistence—particularly among Platonists—on the im-
mortality of his soul. Because of the philosophical difficulties
of this concept, the church had left the matter open as probable, but unsusceptible to proof. In 1513 the Lateran Council
made this belief a dogma of the church.

This responsiveness to demand is shown not only by what
the church allowed but by what it condemned. The most
notorious example of this is the persecution of witches. There
was nothing new about a belief in witches. In a sermon of 1505
at Tübingen, which reads like an encyclopaedic synopsis of
common knowledge, Martin Plantsch reminded his congrega-
tion that witches raised storms, had cats as familiars, caused
impotence, manipulated sickness and health, broke into wine
cellars through closed door, used powders, infusions, images
and desecrated the sacraments. This was familiar folklore.
What was new was sustained official notice. In 1484 Innocent
VIII issued his bull *Summis Desiderantes Affectibus* which
authorised the Dominican inquisitors Heinrich Kramer and
Jacob Sprenger to stamp out witchcraft in Germany. Two
years later they published the founding document of witch
persecution, the *Malleus Maleficarum*, a recognition chart for
witches with directions how to prosecute them which rapidly
gained a European circulation. Innocent's bull, listing the
enormities committed by witches, included damage to crops
and animals, sexual impotence in men and barrenness in
women. By providing scapegoats for a wide range of economic
and personal calamities the church was satisfying appetites
as urgent as those which sought new ways of expressing
a spiritual need.

All the traditional aids to Catholic devotion were enthusias-
tically taken advantage of; indeed, it was in response to the
vigour of these devotions that satire at the expense of super-

allowed the variety of religious experience to cover its walls and crown its altars. And the walls and altars continued to be built.

In France, Spain and Germany there were many new churches and new chapels inserted in old ones. In England, the glass of Fairford and King's College, Cambridge, the tower at Fountains and Bath Abbey are only among the best known examples of an impressive activity in the building of churches and the furnishing of them with tombs, chantries, new pews, pulpits and screens, and with the carved alabaster for which the country was famous. Still more impressive evidence of the continuing vitality of religious observance is found in the activities of the lay confraternities which gave the non-labourer townsman a personal stake in the apparatus and the devotional satisfaction offered by the church. In addition to the social importance of the schools run by some of them and to the charity they extended outside their own membership the confraternities could be notable patrons. In 1517 the Venetian confraternity of S. Rocco began the building of the meeting house (*scuola*) for which Tintoretto was to paint a series of masterpieces spanning his career. In Florence, the confraternity *dello Scalzo* bought land next to their little church for a cloister which Andrea del Sarto began to decorate in 1511 with the most beautiful *grisaille* works of all time. At the other extreme were the little alabaster plaques carrying eucharistic emblems which were sold for a shilling or two to members of the York confraternity of Corpus Christi to keep in their homes.

iv

There were many rungs in the ladder that lead man to God. A window placed in Saint-Laurence in Beauvais in 1516 shows a man who kneels, begging Laurence's intercession; the saint in turn looks beseechingly to the Virgin, who looks to Christ, who looks to God. The number of those who wished to sweep the rungs clean of saintly relics, mariolatrous devotions and

third fairly easily definable group were those English Lollards who continued to keep alive the notions of Wyclif: rejection of transubstantiation, confession, prayers for the dead and clerical celibacy. They distrusted all non-biblical ceremony and stressed the importance of reading the scriptures in the vernacular. Lollard ideas were in the main restricted to poor men. Legally punishable with death if, after conviction and recantation, they relapsed, the English bishops did not pursue the Lollards with fierceness. The numbers involved were small and most of them recanted at the first prosecution. How many men, not Lollards to the extent of being identified as such, were influenced by their arguments against ritual, clerical wealth and exclusiveness and their bitterness against Rome, it is impossible to say.

Outside these sects, each of which possessed (or, in the case of the Lollards, had possessed) some form of 'church' organisation of their own, all over Europe from time to time individuals, moved by some psychic tension, dashed the host to the ground and jumped on it, shouted aloud that the pope was antichrist or announced their intention of begetting a new Saviour. The lack of any firm notion of secular progress, plus the enduring tradition of medieval chiliastic dreams, meant that in moments of political or social stress the wildest forecasts of the coming of Antichrist or the end of the world could be scribbled on the future without appearing inherently unlikely. Mystical excesses led Spanish friars to claim that personal union with God delivered them from the ability to sin and saved them from the responsibility of performing good works. In Germany and the Netherlands similar notions, with enough common psychological and doctrinal ground to relate them to the centuries-old heresy of the Free Spirit, prompted men to claim that the entire organisation of the church was a fraud, that man has the ability to be God and that once he has recognised this is free to make love to his sister or his brother before the altar or to murder his children. Still more common was a simple sticking to the word of the scriptures, and not only among poor and ignorant men; 'I would give two shillings to anyone who could show me any passage in holy writ which

cantation, talismans and spell-like songs, man's spiritual nature. Humanism itself grew from the study of pagan books, but it would be difficult to show that outright paganism was any threat to the church. Little significance need be read into the case of the man who, in 1503 in Paris seized the host from the hands of the priest and declared that 'Jupiter and Hercules are the only true gods.' More significant, and immensely moving, is the account left by Fra Luca della Robbia of the last hours of Pierpaolo Boscoli, sentenced to death for his involvement in an assassination plot against the Medici in 1513. 'Rid me,' he pleaded, 'of the memory of Brutus, so that I may die a Christian.' The friar claimed that after wrestling all night to rescue Boscoli from the values of his humanist education he succeeded. And doubtless this is true. Given the religious temper of the age it was a very rare man whose last moments were filled by a vision of the Elysian Fields rather than of the Christian judgement day.

The study of antiquity could lead to more dispassionate views about the merit of other religious systems than the Christian. Thus Machiavelli could praise the valorous patriotism that Roman religion gave the soldiers of the Republic, thus Mutianus Rufus, who had been a classmate of Erasmus in the 1480s, could teach that the philosophy of the ancients and the religions of the Jews and of the Christians were but different reflections of the steady outpouring of God's divinity. And this comparative approach could shade into deism, as in Celtis:

> *'You marvel that I never move my lips in any church,*
> *Murmuring through my teeth in prayer.*
> *The reason is that the great divine will of Heaven*
> *Hears the small inner voice.*
> *You marvel that you so seldom see me*
> *Dragging my feet into the temples of the gods.*
> *God is within us. I do not need to meditate on Him*
> *In painted churches.'*

But there was seldom any doubt as to where the priority lay

# CHAPTER VII

# THE ARTS AND THEIR AUDIENCE

i

When da Gama's men went on shore after rounding the Cape of Good Hope they were greeted by natives playing a kind of flute, 'thus making a pretty harmony for negroes who are not expected to be musicians'. It was to be expected, however, that the seamen would be able to answer in kind, and they did. The early voyagers took trumpets and drums which were used to assist company keeping and to give signals in fog but also for recreation. Erasmus was not indulging in sentiment when he expressed the hope that New Testament stories would be sung at the spinning wheel and the plough. Music, from the simplest unaccompanied song to the choirs of cathedrals and the orchestras of princely courts, provided the most widely shared and, arguably at least, the most deeply felt of cultural pleasures.

No description of the feelings induced by looking at a work of art had the intensity of Andrea Calmo's reaction to a concert; 'as for the manner of singing, I have never heard anything better. God! what a beautiful voice, what style, what fullness, what diminuendoes, what suavity that would melt the hardest hearts.' Dürer noted that in Venice, in the course of another concert, the viol players themselves were moved to tears, and one of Leo X's chapel masters, Elzéar Genêt, resolved to renounce secular music altogether because of the danger of arousing the wrong passions too strongly. In similar vein a German prayerbook of 1509, accepting that its readers would 'sing during your work in house and field, at your seasons of prayer and devotion, in times of joy and in times of sorrow', added: 'good songs are agreeable to God, bad ones are sinful and must be avoided.' To elevate the mind, to ease the working day: the power, the utility, the universal popularity of music were taken for granted in a way notably different from

treaty, and most towns of any size employed a town band of trumpeters, fife-players and drummers. In Antwerp they even gave regular evening concerts. But there is an abundance of evidence to show that music was taken for granted in the home as well. From 1501 printed music began to appear, much of it divided into separate books so that each performer could have his own part before him; dedications show that a great part of this printed music, both vocal and instrumental, was intended for private homes.

The pace for changes in style and expertise of execution was set by the orchestras and vocalists attached, as a matter of course, to noble households. There was much competition for the services of composers and instrumentalists; singers at the papal court under Leo X could command salaries at least as high as those paid to men of letters. Lorenzo de' Medici placed a memorial to the 'family' musician Squarcialupi in the Florentine cathedral. Maximilian actually knighted his court organist, Paul Hofheimer. It is not at all out of keeping with the prestige of music among the other arts that Leonardo, in a famous letter in which he attempted to recommend himself to Lodovico Sforza of Milan, while setting out his competence as painter, sculptor and military engineer, gave special prominence to his ability as a lute player. Leo X himself composed music, as did Henry VIII. A list of princes and monarchs who could play an instrument would indeed be wearisome, and the point is only worth making because there was none who could paint or sculpt or—with the possible exception of Lorenzo de' Medici, who submitted a design for the unfinished façade of the cathedral in Florence—had any competence as an architect. The plethora of music-making angels in art, the use of musical instruments as a theme in *intarsia* work, Raphael's S. Cecilia (formerly a rare subject), the existence of music academies, in the sense of performing and discussion groups, in Siena and Rome: these examples are a reminder of the part music played in a culture which has become famous in retrospect chiefly for the visual arts.

In Italy the emphasis in court music was above all secular, though some princes took a close interest in the quality of the

oriented musicians of the north, and the existence of such centres as Milan, Florence, Mantua, Ferrara and Urbino offered a wider range of secular patronage than was available there. Obrecht, Isaac and Josquin all worked for a while in Florence.

Thanks to the printing press, the correspondence of music-ally minded humanists and the competition between courts and churches, the names and the personalities of players, singers and composers were widely known and discussed. The emphasis on instrumental improvisation, the emergence of a vocal connoisseurship in which the quality of an individual voice was matter for eager discussion: these factors, too, worked to a similar effect. Increasingly composers signed their works. Ockeghem's death in 1495 was mourned not only in works by fellow composers but in an epitaph by Erasmus. As in the other arts, there was a self-conscious attempt to break from earlier traditions, particularly from the deeply en-trenched Gregorian chant, the principle of successive com-position (as opposed to harmonic composition, in which the parts were imagined simultaneously) and the subordination of the sense of the words to the pattern of the music. And against the background of this desire for novelty, composers stood out in stronger personal relief, as in an Italian letter com-paring Isaac with Josquin des Prez and praising the former more highly because 'he will compose new things more often'. And disputes between rival theorists helped to sustain the notion of music as an evolving art form. That between the Spaniard Bartolomé Ramos de Pareja and Franchino Gaffurio, who held the chair of music at Milan and was also director of music at the cathedral, led to a widespread taking of sides, especially when the dispute sank to the level of personal abuse, with Ramos accusing Gaffurio of not only being a bastard and a drunkard but of having a voice like a raven.

Interest, opportunity, itinerancy, printing: these help to explain the speed of diffusion of one of the chief advances of the period—thinking in terms of chords rather than of successively added layers. But the creation of a harmonic

musician-painters: music had obvious links with learning and
the other arts. Its emotionalism may have reflected the desire
for a more personal religion, the emphasis on music following meaning almost certainly reflected the humanists' emphasis on the properly established text and their knowledge that
Greek music had been closely moulded to the poems it enhanced. In imagining the effect of a score as a whole rather
than as an accumulation of detail, composers were running in
parallel to the practice of painters and sculptors. The links
can be sensed more readily than they can be identified, but
there can be little doubt that the extent to which men were
coming to think of 'culture', of their relationship to the product of a number of forms of creative expression, was primarily
determined by music. Numerically, more men and women
listened to music and made it than was true of any other art.
Qualitatively, the actual effect of music on the individual
appears to have been greater. The 'all round' man was encouraged by his education to be aware of all the arts, of culture
as a whole, but it was more likely to be through the lute than
through brush or chisel that he would gain any practical experience of the formal and technical problems all forms of
advanced art have in common.

ii

Second only to music in the number of people it affected,
and the extent to which it moved them was the drama. The
range of dramatic entertainment was wide. At one end of the
scale was the dramatic monologue, a single actor telling a
story or giving a mock sermon or impersonating a variety of
characters and voices in what amounted to a one-man play. At
the other was the street pageant which could involve changing the appearance of thoroughfares and squares and might
employ a sizeable proportion of the population as extras. In the
same way that great men maintained their own orchestras,
they kept troupes of actors, usually small, from four to ten;
like orchestras, these troupes could be lent to other notables or

machinery for getting the plot under way, and one or two of the characters owe a debt to Plautus. Even more interesting in showing how readily classical models could be updated into contemporary terms is the same author's slightly later comedy, *Clizia*, for while this is firmly based on Plautus' *Casina*, the tone is that of 1506, the year in which Machiavelli places it, and the play splendidly exemplifies his belief that 'the aim of a comedy is to hold up a mirror to domestic life'. No other source gives so realistic an account of a day in the life of an early sixteenth century Florentine bourgeois than the speech in which Sofronia laments her husband's infatuation with a young girl.

'Anyone who knew Nicomaco a year ago and came across him today couldn't help being amazed by the great change that's come over him. He used to be thought dignified, respon-sible, sober. He passed his time worthily; got up early in the morning, heard Mass, ordered the day's food, and then saw to whatever business he had in town, at the market or the magistrates' office. If not, he either discussed some serious topic or other with a few friends or shut himself in his study at home to balance and tidy up his accounts. Then he dined happily with his family and after dinner talked to his son, gave him advice, helped him understand human nature, taught him how to live, in fact, with examples from past and present. Then he went out and spent the rest of the day either in business or in some sober and respectable recreation. Every evening he was home by dark, stayed with us a while by the fire if it was winter, then went into his study to look over his affairs, and three hours after sunset he had supper in the best of humours . . . But since he's had this girl on the brain, his affairs have been neglected, his farms are decaying, his trade going to ruin. He's always criticising, and doesn't know why; he comes in and out of the house a thousand times a day without knowing what he's meant to be doing, and at meal-times he's never there. If you speak to him he doesn't answer, or his answer is right off the point. The servants see this going on and laugh at him, and his son has lost all respect for him.'

emitted sparks. To the same effect auditions were held for gild mysteries in order to achieve a convincing level of acting and clerics could obtain permission to grow beards while preparing their parts.

The rapid alternations between tragic and ribald moments in the mystery, which had been a traditional feature of their writing and took for granted an emotionally volatile audience in whom tears and guffaws could alternate quickly and naturally, gave little scope for psychological realism: the broad effect was the aim. However, there was a tendency to clarify the action by having more dialogue in fewer scenes, to develop characters in a life-like manner and to play down the element of the merely grotesque or the purely miraculous. In 1486, for instance, Jehan Michel undertook to up-date an earlier version of the Angers passion play. He lopped off the Old Testament scenes, eliminated one in which the purpose of salvation was debated (as being too rarified and scholastic), added spice to the character of Judas by making him kill his father and marry his mother and added pathos to that of the Magdalen. After questioning those who had already seen Jesus about his age, complexion and the colour of his eyes, she decides to seduce him and goes to hear him teach in her most alluring costume. After trying in vain to attract his attention she falls under the spell of his words and his message and, moved by guilt and repentance dissolves into tears. Describing the comparable Alsfeld passion (1501), Kuno Franke wrote that 'in characters and scenes like these, the Christian legend, we feel, has come to be entirely acclimatised to German city life . . . it has come to be a perfect expression of the personal experience of the average citizen of those days.'*

The organisation of the mystery play was largely in the hands of the average citizen, though it may have been written or modified by a learned cleric. All gild or craft members responsible for particular scenes or series of episodes were expected to help pay for them. The timing of their performance, commonly once a year, was also determined by moments of

* *Personality in German Literature before Luther* (Harvard, 1916) 137.

Charles—to the mystery and the pageant, a very large proportion of the men who commissioned, or simply looked at
paintings and sculpture, together with the artists themselves,
were familiar with at least some forms of dramatic entertainment.


iii


The connection between artists and the drama is in one sense
straightforward. Andrea del Sarto painted theatrical sets,
Leonardo produced pageant designs, Pontormo decorated some
of the triumphal cars with which Florence celebrated the news
of Giovanni de' Medici's elevation to the papacy as Leo X
in 1513. The mystery of the passion produced twice a year in
Vienna was directed by the prominent sculptor Rollinger.
Dürer's Triumphal Arch woodcut was the echo on a flamboyant scale of the specially constructed arches where visiting
potentates received addresses of welcome.

Less straightforward is the connection between the drama
and the overall effect of the visual arts. There was a com-
parability of effect, at least, between the *tableaux vivants* of
actors posed against a painted background which were dispersed along a pageant route and the way in which painters
placed their characters—in an Annunciation, a Birth of the
Virgin or a Last Supper—in an enclosed space. The feeling
for unity and enclosure is very similar. In all likelihood the
feeling for unity of setting had originally passed from painting to the stage, but it is possible that an interest in psychological realism had passed the other way, that painters had
been aided in their expression of grief or anguish or expectancy by watching actors. A more important link, perhaps, was
the attitude not of those who produced but those who paid for
works of art. All, again, whether wealthy individuals, gilds or
city fathers, were used to seeing men acting in the familiar
stories of the bible or the lives of the saints, or in the morali-
ties and secular farces. They were used, in fact, to looking
carefully at actual bodies in repose or movement, as though

which inculcate wantonness, vainglory or tyranny.' And Cortese, writing his description of how the ideal cardinal should live, stressed that in his bedroom he should only hang pictures which should provide him with some virtuous subject for meditation as he opened his eyes.

One source of a general interest in the arts was civic pride. Cristoforo Landino in 1481 cited Florence's painters and architects as one cause for the city's great repute. Felix Faber, writing about a new church in his description of Ulm, his own city, proudly remarked that 'it is larger than any other parish church...and more majestic than most cathedrals' and, though he does not dare compare it with Santa Sophia in Constantinople, nevertheless 'our church is more beautiful than all others.' And he went on to cite a third reason for its uniqueness: 'there are more altars here than in all other parish churches, for it has fifty-one altars, all well provided and fully recognised; and they are fitted out not by princes or strangers but by the citizens of Ulm themselves.'

This system of allocating chapels and altars to individual families or to gilds and lay confraternities did much to extend an interest in the paintings and sculpture with which they were furnished. Patronage was not restricted to the clergy responsible for a particular church, but extended fairly widely into the community, from patricians to artisans. In some places gilds were made responsible for the upkeep of a church as a whole, its furnishing and alteration, and as gild officials commonly served on a rotating basis, this extended the number of individuals who would have to make a decision bearing on a work of art. Possibly public taste was educated by municipal commissions like the decoration of the Hall of the Great Council of Venice in 1480; that such commissions were sometimes open to public competition (the design of a façade for the Florentine cathedral in 1489 is an example) was another occasion for general comment and debate.

The rival workshops themselves, largely family concerns, but taking on youths from outside who wished to become painters or sculptors, acted as stimuli to keeping abreast with change. Moreover, though some works, portraits in the main,

for some years mechanically satisfied—it is likely that even in art centres like Florence, Antwerp or Vienna the number of men capable of being actually moved by a painting or other work of art for its own sake was far smaller than those who could be affected by music or the drama. On the other hand the degree of familiarity with what was going on meant that artists were dealing with a tolerant audience capable of taking stylistic change and personal eccentricity in its stride. The period 1480–1520 saw crucial changes in the painting, sculpture and architecture of Italy, France, Germany and the Netherlands, significant ones in England and Spain and at least isolated changes in Poland and Russia. But there was virtually no vandalism, no public outcry. It is not known what paintings (if any), drawings and prints perished in the Savonarolan bonfires of vanities. The protest was, in any case, against lascivious subject matter, not against any novelty of style.

The acceptance of works of art in public places was aided by their subject matter. Treatment changed, but the themes —saints and nativities in churches, political allegories and portraits in town halls—remained familiar. Scenes from ancient history and mythology were painted for the homes of individual enthusiasts. Though sarcophagi and other fragments of Roman statuary were to be seen in the towns of Italy and southern France, and though every pilgrim to Rome could see the collection of classical sculpture on the Capitol which Sixtus IV had opened to the public, the infrequency of prints and the absence of really clumsy paintings of classical subjects suggests that only the well-to-do chose to commission classical themes. Again, if there was little in the public domain to startle through its subject matter, there was also no significantly new demand made on the intellect. So far from playing down the symbolic content of medieval art, the increasing mastery of realism among the painters of the fifteenth century made the use of symbols even more exact and complex. No medieval work included so many symbolic objects as did Dürer's Melancolia engraving, nor so many allusions to layers of meaning as can be teased out of Leonardo's Last

foreshadowed, by events in the Old was a commonplace of sermons and devotional literature and had been given wide circulation through such illustrated books as the so-called *Bible of the Poor* and the *Mirror of Human Salvation*. This is not to say that the average pilgrim would have caught the nature of Michelangelo's personal involvement or of the intellectual programme that helped him to give visual unity to the ceiling scheme as a whole. It is probable, however, that the mastery of naturalistic techniques combined with the continuing habit of assuming that everything could stand for something else either as a symbol (the rabbit for sensuality) or as a personification (David as courage powered by a sense of right) or as an allegory (the scarlet feather of the goldfinch clasped in the Christ child's hand an anticipation of the blood of the passion), led to a religious art more meaningful than any that had preceded it. The urge to identification through psychological and physical realism was catered for without alienating the mystical temperament that sought for deeper and deeper meanings under mere appearance.

Really esoteric art was largely restricted to Italy, was secular (the paintings of Bosch are a rare example of a minority, possibly 'secret' approach to religion finding visual expression) and outside the public domain. The humanist interest in rare texts and Hermetic and hieroglyphic *curiosa* led to a proliferation of images that could be understoood only by the highly cultivated, by those who could spot the classical reference or see the appropriateness of an image to a specific individual. For the most part these works were medals, designed to be exchanged among friends and equals, or plaquettes. And even they sprang naturally, though in antique guise, from the heraldic habit of identifying the essence of an individual in a crest and a motto.

Such designs were not left to the sculptor or goldsmith. Indeed, with very few exceptions, such as technical exercises like the Medusa's head attributed by Vasari to Leonardo or the 'fake' antique cupid similarly attributed to the young Michelangelo, all paintings and works of sculpture were the result of direct commission. Monasteries, confraternities, gilds,

grouping and setting. Jean Perréal and Jean Clouet were the portraitists favoured by the French court because they seemed to strike the right note between naturalism and decorum. The wealthy merchants of Augsburg supported Hans Burgkmair because his work had the Italian flavour which was then becoming fashionable. And in urban centres with an educated court or bourgeoisie the favour of patrons was likely to be given to those slightly ahead of stylistic tradition.

Modishness, no doubt, played a part in this. Men who went to great pains to procure the latest fashions in clothing and armour were likely to wish to be pace-setters in their artistic purchases as well. More important, however, was the fact that certain of the stylistic intentions that led to change were well suited to reflect attitudes that had been formed by the education and manner of life of wealthy and influential men. This was above all true of Italy. By the late fifteenth century painters and sculptors were in a position to draw together the threads of the experimental and sometimes quirkish generations that had preceded them: experiments in perspective, anatomy, emotional expressiveness, monumentality. During those same generations, under the influence of humanism (meaning, in this context, chiefly the ideas of Cicero and Quintilian and the *Lives* of Plutarch) and, to a lesser extent, of chivalry, the governing class had evolved a newly self-conscious image of itself. With due allowance for difference of place and function this image emphasised a glossing over of vocational preoccupations, a spacious hospitality to ideas, an imperturbable confidence in the face of adversity and a calculated ease of manner, a carrying lightly of varied accomplishments.

In the course of the late fifteenth and early sixteenth centuries the evolution of style in art led to a fairly close echoing of this style in life. There was a seeking for the broad, spatially coherent effect, an absence of fussiness, a concealment of the means whereby the overall impression had been gained, a portraiture that (master now of straightforward copying from nature) sought to reveal the working of the intellect; the human figure, supremely at ease whether in an archi-

were by now common property. It is likely that behind the
bleak bones of a contract we should see conversations in which
patron and artist, with or without the intervention of a
learned go-between, would discuss not only the subject of a
painting but to some extent the spirit in which it was to be
executed.

Artists were literate men. In 1503 Leonardo possessed one
hundred and sixteen books, an unusually large library for any
private individual, and while most of these were concerned
with conveying information, about medicine and mathematics,
for example, he had books of poetry, including Pulci and
Burchiello, and examples of the most popular form of contemporary escape literature, the chivalric romance. Though
this was an exceptional case, the workshop, with its variety of
occupations from coats of arms and trousseau chests to monuments and fresco cycles, was a lively environment, not far
removed in mood from the printer's shop—to which, through
engraving and woodcut it might, indeed, be linked. Personal
rivalry among apprentices and inter-workshop rivalry gave an
edge to an artist's training, an edge sharpened by the challenge
of new techniques like painting in oil instead of tempera (still
unusual in Italy in the 1480s) or drawing in chalks and by the
desire for self-education beyond the training available in the
workshop. The example in the middle of the fifteenth century
of Leon Battista Alberti, who combined noble blood, humanist scholarship and executive brilliance as an architect and
sculptor, had been of enduring importance. He had written
treatises on painting, sculpture and architecture. He had
shown that art could be learned and that learned men could,
indeed should, take an interest in the arts. The result was to
encourage the artist's increasing sense of the importance of his
own personality and the intellectual value of his calling. Travel
for the purpose of improving technique and absorbing the
atmosphere of a more advanced milieu—the motives which
took Dürer to Venice and Raphael from Urbino to Florence—
became more frequent. But artists sought to cultivate their
minds as well in the service of their art. Raphael was considered competent to draw up a report on the condition of the

been to provide an advertisement for the artist's workshop rather than simply proclaim the work as his own. Another indication of increased self-confidence was the practice, particularly common in Italy, of including a self-portrait in a picture or fresco, or, more rarely, a small scale replica of one of the artist's own paintings. Dürer's preoccupation with himself and his progress was reflected in a series of independent self-portraits, beginning with a drawing at the age of thirteen, and in the consistency with which he dated his engravings.

By means of engravings and drawings, the travels of artists and the increasing traffic of diplomats and soldier-patrons to Italy after 1494, Italian ideas became diffused throughout the rest of Europe. The export of Italian paintings was not very important in this period; far more influential was the sending of Raphael's tapestry cartoons—supreme representations of the 'high' style—to Brussels, where the actual weaving was to be done. The atelier in which they were housed became for a while the Brancacci chapel of the north. But one of the reasons why Italian visual ideas were accepted was that they did *not* all represent this style. The degree of individual and regional difference in the peninsula—some due to the import of northern works and the employment of northern painters earlier in the fifteenth century—made it possible for artists to borrow from Italy according to their own needs.

The process of diffusion was slow and by no means uniform. In cities like Nuremberg, Munich and Cracow, for example, where a native tradition in sculpture was still evolving strongly according to its own rules, the Italian example was rejected. In Antwerp Italian painting failed to appeal to painters who were working out a novel manner of their own. Moreover there was a quite widespread move in the Netherlands to reinvigorate art by a return to the principles underlying *their* great masters of the early fifteenth century, Van Eyck, the Master of Flemalle and Petrus Christus. In Germany Grünewald, though unmistakably a painter of the early sixteenth century, drew his inspiration from looking back to the devotional art of the late fourteenth century rather than across to Italy. Indeed, the serenity which characterised the bulk of

Fouquet had painted—in enamel—his self-portrait, possibly
indicates something like the personal self-consciousness so
common in Italy. Perréal prided himself on being a poet and
on having some knowledge of astronomy and philosophy; but
he had what was possibly a unique personal acquaintance with
artists in Italy. It is doubtful that among non-Italian artists
as a whole there was either the desire for or the ability to take
advantage of the educational process taken for granted in
Italy. The fame that Fra Bartolommeo gained for himself and
the workshop in the monastery of S. Marco in Florence which
he directed, is in sharp contrast to the diagnosis offered by a
fellow friar of Hugo van der Goes' attacks of pathological
depression: 'since he was only human—as are all of us—the
various honours, visits and accolades that came to him made
him feel very important. Thus, since God did not want him
to perish, He in His compassion sent him this humiliating
disease which indeed made him very contrite.'

And if the educational atmosphere in which painters and
sculptors worked outside Italy made it difficult for them to
sympathise with the principles underlying Italian art, the difficulty was still greater for achitects. Outside Italy, architecture was largely in the hands of men trained as masons and
serving their apprenticeship in the great cathedrals which
were still being built in the Gothic style, Cologne and Tours
among them, or in Gothic parish churches such as the one so
praised by Felix Fabri. Most of the influential Italian architects were, on the other hand, men who had never been
trained to place one stone upon another. Bramante, Raphael,
Michelangelo all were invited to turn to architecture after
establishing themselves as painters. Fra Giocondo started as a
scholar. Only Giuliano and Antonio da San Gallo appear to
have been professional architects from an early age.

In Italy, therefore, architects inherited the theoretical interests considered appropriate to painters and the conditioning of painting itself by architectural settings which could
afford to be pedantically classical because nobody but painted
people had to live in them. In practice they looked chiefly to
the sturdy regional architecture of the peninsula and to the

# CHAPTER VIII

# SECULAR LEARNING

i

By origin the study of ancient texts, by extension an educational programme based on certain of them, particularly those concerned with history, moral philosophy and rhetoric: by the late fifteenth century it is possible to describe humanism as a state of mind. Alongside the discovery and editing of texts, and the use of them as educational tools, the outlines of a great civilisation had emerged, vast in extent and time. No doubt the rise and decline first of Athens and then of Rome had reflected the Christian God's will, but the Greeks and Romans had been unaware of it, and this enabled those who disinterred and read their narratives to see antiquity in its own terms. The present had come, as it were, to possess an *alter ego*. In addition to the inhabitants of the heavenly city of God, men could now imagine a society like their own, lacking only the compass, printing, gunpowder, the papacy and the Americas: a society which, thanks to time's winnowing of its more trivial sources and monuments, appeared to have been peopled by an intellectual and creative master-race. Whatever there was to do, in philosophical speculation, political action or cultural achievement appeared to have been done, and done with a supreme vigour and accomplishment, among a people whose history not only had the clarity of distance in time but the wholeness of a completed cycle, from obscurity through world empire to barbarian chaos.

Text by text, as the imaginative reconstruction of the ancient world proceeded, the relevance of this *alter ego* had become clearer. Their words no longer obscure, their personalities restored, replaced in the context of their own society, the appeal of the authors the middle ages had known, Plato, Aristotle, Virgil, Cicero and Ovid, became stronger than ever,

nature but by the readiness of individuals and societies to accept them, and that readiness was quickened by the evidence of creative vigour in native vernacular culture as well as in classical scholarship. Florence was experiencing a 'golden age' because the Italian poetry of Lorenzo de' Medici, the sculpture of Verrochio and Benedetto da Maiano and the painting of Botticelli, Filippino Lippi and many others proved a breadth of vitality which could take advantage of the advice proffered from antiquity. Von Hutten, in a letter to Pirckheimer in 1518, referring to the Frenchmen Lefèvre and Budé and to the humanists of his own country, exclaimed 'Oh century! Oh letters! It is a joy to be alive! Studies thrive and minds flourish! Woe to you, Barbarians! Accept the noose, look forward to exile!' His optimism was buoyed up by Germany's greatest surge of creative vigour in literature and the arts before the eighteenth century. Educated in the Low Countries at a time when the church music of the Netherlands was an example to the rest of Europe, later a friend of Holbein, Erasmus, too, was expressing a hope that the humanities would refresh the quality of life at a time when the tide of creativity was running high; 'the world is coming to its senses as if awaking out of a deep sleep.'

For Erasmus and von Hutten humanism was a calling in of the wisdom of the old world to redress the values of the new. In northern Europe, the values that were felt most to need correction were those that concerned the religious life. Referring to the teaching of the New Testament, Erasmus emphasised that 'this sort of philosophy is rather a matter of disposition than of syllogisms, rather of life than of disputation . . . Moreover, though no one has taught this so absolutely and effectively as Christ, yet also in pagan books much may be found that is in accordance with it.' He was expressing what Ficino and Pico had written about more esoterically and Raphael—through the room in the Vatican where The Dispute about the Sacrament faced The School of Athens— had expressed in paint. It was primarily the Italian humanists' search for an accord between the teaching of the ancients and of Christ that enabled classical studies to be accepted as

the honour of being practised by people of free birth, and
later on by persons of station, it having always been forbidden
that slaves should be instructed in it', and that Apelles was
so favoured by Alexander the Great that he handed over his
mistress Campaspe, with whom the artist had fallen in love
when painting her in the nude. And chiming harmoniously
with the humanist emphasis on man as creator, the importance
of the artist's genius as well as the finished product of his
hand, was Pliny's statement that in antiquity 'the last works
of artists and their unfinished pictures ... are more admired
than those which they finished, because in them one sees the
preliminary drawings left visible and the artist's actual
thoughts.' Whether it was a defence of the nude, scorn for
the use of expensive pigments merely for ostentation, or the
inclusion of a portrait of his mistress in a sacred picture, the
painter could find confirmation of what he was already
doing and an affirmation of the liberal status of his profession.
It is, of course, easier to show relevance than to demonstrate
effect but at least this example suggests the encouragement
given by the popularisation of humanistic studies, an encouragement expressed in a very different context by Cortes'
exhortation to his little band of Spanish adventurers to imitate
the heroic deeds of the Romans; whereupon, his chronicler,
Diaz, records, 'to a man we all responded that we would do his
orders, that the die was cast for good fortune, as Caesar said at
the Rubicon.'

The wide appeal of antiquity was dependent on parallels between the nature of ancient and contemporary society. In war
and politics the parallel was (except for gunpowder) fairly
close. It held good for the rôle of the writer and orator, the
lawyer and doctor, and for certain occupations, particularly that of the farmer. That the philosopher and the scien-
tist had much to learn is obvious. More difficult to estimate
is the effect of noticing differences between the two cultures.
The ancient world depended on a substratum of slaves; did
this increase the scorn felt by humanist writers for the lowest
grades of their own society? It was anti-feminist: did this
influence the increasing subordination of the serious role of

his defenders, von Hutten and Crotus Rubeanus, were not content with this and in the following year published a pendant, the *Letters of Obscure Men*. This purported to be a selection of letters written to one of Reuchlin's chief adversaries, Ortvinus Gratius, a theologian at the University of Cologne, by his admirers. With considerable skill and great relish these 'admirers' made it clear that Ortvinus was an immoral and pettifogging ignoramus. They celebrated his sordid amours, praised his ability to determine such weighty matters as whether the eating of an egg containing an unhatched chick on a Friday were a venial or a mortal sin, and, above all, they impugned his learning. 'When I was in your study at Cologne' wrote one of them in mock respect, 'I could see well enough that you had a multitude of volumes, both great and small. Some were clad in wooden boards, and some in parchment bindings, some were covered all over with leather, red and green and black, while some were half bound. And there you sat, with a whisk in your hand, to flap away the dust from the bindings.'

This passive respect for authority attributed to Ortvinus and his like was in strong contrast to the use made of books by his assailants. The printing press was, indeed, crucial to the diffusion of humanist ideas. Governments were in general encouraging. John II of Portugal licensed book imports in 1483 'because it is good for the commonwealth to have many books circulating in our kingdom'. Louis XII referred to printing in an ordinance of 1513 as 'a divine rather than human invention'. The number of cities with presses of their own varied from country to country: in 1500 there were seventy-three such centres in Italy, fifty in Germany, forty-five in France and four in England. And the export of books was well organised. Printed texts enabled scholars in different countries to quote passages by page and chapter. By selecting with little discrimination what medieval works were to be put into circulation, printing had, in its first two generations, 'fixed' the image of medieval culture. It thus played into the hands of the humanists who could represent it as an undifferentiated pile of superstition and frivolity which obscured a clear

of Cicero, broadened the range of what was thought to be the appropriate content of informal communication between friends.

ii

The intellectual excitement, the range of important human concerns which looked for illumination to what was in a deeper sense than were the Americas a 'New World' to the late fifteenth and early sixteen centuries, the popularisation of scholarship in the form of classical 'Christian' names, pageantry and decorative clichés: it is tempting to see humanism, by now a fashion as well as a syllabus, as the dominant theme in secular learning. To control this temptation we shall look at its contribution to religion, political thought and science, but there is a question that must be asked first: how pervasive, in fact, was humanism? What was its place within the educational system? Indeed, how many Europeans could be said to have been sufficiently educated to have had any intellectual life at all?

Only vague generalisations can be made about the extent of literacy. The clergy, secular and regular could all, in theory at least, read and write and had been trained to study. Episcopal visitations and reports on monasteries, however, suggest that especially in rural areas there were many priests and monks who were too ignorant to understand the services they read, too uncertainly literate to have their minds extended by reading. Among the labouring poor, the largest single element in the population, the ability to read was probably well under one per cent, the number of those able to write as well very small indeed. Peasants' sons who did go to school and showed promise there were likely to leave the country for the church or for town life. Men of substance in the country could commonly read and write and keep accounts. The proportion of those who could read and write in the towns was much higher; Thomas More thought that something like sixty per cent of Londoners could, and in a city like Florence the proportion may have been higher

cancel out the access a youth would otherwise have had to humanist literature. Rich men, and almost all of those who were of aristocratic birth, preferred to employ a tutor, and in this case the chances of mental curiosity being aroused were much greater unless the father had a prejudice against 'book-learning' as being something best left to poor men's sons who wanted to enter the church.

The great majority of schools were day schools, and this cut down the number of poor country boys who could attend unless they could stay for nothing with a relative—commonly a priest—in a large village or town which possessed one. On the other hand, it meant that the cost of a simple education was small; it was not uncommon for rural schoolmasters to accept fees in kind, in wood or farm produce. At universities, as well as the fees payable to the individual lecturers, money had to be found for board and lodging as well. Most universities had ways of aiding the poor students. They acted as servants in the households of doctors and masters or in the halls of residence, fees could be loaned, waived or reduced. The low proportion of students classified as 'poor', however (sixteen per cent at Cologne, only nine at Leipzig), suggests that many youths even in these circumstances were unable to go to a university. The course, commonly began at the age of fourteen or fifteen, theoretically followed the traditional trivium—grammar, dialectic and rhetoric (all prepared for in elementary fashion at school) and quadrivium—arithmetic, geometry, astronomy and the theory of music. This was the essential preliminary to specialised doctoral work in theology, canon and civil law or medicine.

The days when one man could be master of many subjects was long past. Though universities were remarkably uniform in organisation, intense specialisation had resulted in their having a different tone and balance in the first degree curriculum and, still more, in their reputations at the doctoral level which it was essential for a youth seeking a professional career—including university teaching—or preferment in the church to reach. Thus Bologna and Ferrara were particularly

aim of education was a training of the mind which would be useful in a variety of avocations; they existed to turn out experts. Yet this is not to say that the universities lacked intellectual excitement. The considerable role played by students themselves in the running of university affairs; the encouragement of good teachers by the fact that they were frequently dependent on fees paid direct to them; the practice of itinerancy and the ease of enrolment in different universities; the possibility for independent and unorthodox teachers to set up shop, as it were, in university towns; inter-faculty rivalry, splits in individual faculties, as between the Realist and Nominalist wings of the arts faculties at Ingolstadt and Heidelberg: these were all factors that helped give life to a system unreformed in essentials for more than two centuries.

The point is worth stressing. Under the combative and highly readable onslaught of the humanists, it is easy to forget the vigour and subtlety that could be the product of the scholastic method—lecture and disputation, text books written in terms of questions, answers and qualifications. Under the widening shadow of Reform, it is tempting to dismiss the philosophy and theology of the universities as trivial and sterile. As a moral judgement this is probably fair, but though without the stimulus of thinkers of the originality and power of a William of Occam or an Aquinas, the intellectual standard of these faculties was, in the main, high. Again with Reform in mind, it is easy to agree with the most sweeping criticism of all those levelled against the universities of this period: that Nominalism (chiefly in the north) and a revived Aristotelianism (chiefly in Italy), by dismantling the Thomist harmony between faith and reason, had led to an emasculation of theology because the ordinary processes of argument could not 'prove' religious beliefs, and to a philosophy that had no bearing on a man's inner life. But this had little to do with the training of the mind. Before turning to the humanistic attack on the universities and the attitudes they stood for it is worth remembering that thinkers as creative as Pico and Ficino, More, Erasmus, Guicciardini and Lefèvre d'Étaples were all the products of orthodox higher education, and that

that He had been scattering clues to His nature and His intentions through the writings of non-Jewish antiquity, so that, properly studied, the works of Plato could give spiritual, just as those of Cicero could give ethical, guidance. These last goals led to a re-appraisal of a few school and university syllabuses in the cause of harmonising the noblest messages from antiquity with the least riddling statements of scripture.

Humanism, then, had a mystical core, exemplified by such men as Pico, Colet and Lefèvre, a secondary circle of men like Erasmus and More whose leanings were predominantly moral, and an outer circle of popularisers whose inclination varied between the practical pedagogy of Linacre to the unconscious cynicism of Castiglione. All were sustained in their enthusiasm by a genuine love of the languages of antiquity, particularly Latin (for a mastery of Greek was still an uncommon accomplishment) and a desire to purify it in the teeth of the general run of teachers who, as Celtis put it, 'speak from their Chairs brokenly and crudely against all art and rule of speech like hissing geese or lowing oxen, pouring forth common, vile and corrupt words and whatever enters their mouths, pronouncing harshly and barbarously the smooth Latin tongue.'

The attack on teaching methods went closest to the heart of current practice. Throughout the trivium and quadrivium and to a lesser extent in doctoral studies, logic played so great a part that in the worst instances, at least, individual disciplines were exploited as fodder for the primary activity of debate and problem solving, ingenuity being put well above understanding, epitomes of quotations above the texts from which they were culled. Against this practice the humanists emphasised the need to study texts as a whole, together with an analysis of their style and a knowledge of the times in which they were written. The purpose was to understand a writer in terms of why, how and when he wrote. In terms of the *trivium* this meant a playing down of grammar and dialectic and a radical up-grading of rhetoric—the study of literature and philosophy in order to understand what great men actually said and to be able to speak and write eloquently and pertinently oneself. For the great advantage of rhetoric in this new

in Petrarch's feeling for Cicero. The editing of Latin and, to a lesser extent, Greek texts had been one of the chief preoccupations of humanists throughout the fifteenth century. In the deliberations of governments, besides, and in the fad for genealogy, a strong instinct to look back to origins was making iself felt: in many areas the intellectual drive of the period can be summed up in the phrase *reculer pour mieux sauter*. More revolutionary—for the scale on which the argument was pressed rather than for its originality—was the determination to get back past the scholastic theologians to the Bible itself and to the early fathers of the church, 'the old doctors who were nigh unto Christ and his apostles', as Erasmus put it.

In 1496 Colet's lectures at Oxford on St. Paul's Epistles to the Corinthians broke radically with the traditional methods of the divinity teacher. Instead of approaching his subject through medieval Latin commentaries, thus reminding his auditors that the church represented an accumulation of interpretations as well as of dogma, he used the Greek text directly. He explained how the form and language of the Epistles were conditioned by St. Paul's view of the men to whom it was directed. He placed Paul himself within the context of Roman civilisation and the early years of Christianity. And by locating him clearly in place and time Colet enabled Paul to speak almost as directly to the students of Oxford as he had spoken to the Corinthians—to bear witness from the beginnings of the church and to encourage personal reflection instead of being used as the excuse for a display of erudition. Perhaps even more impressive as exemplifying the humanistic desire to return to the sources was the desire to see the Bible in what was essentially the language of God and Christ, Hebrew. Pico studied the language: Reuchlin formulated its rules so that others could study it. But it is once more from Erasmus that we see their motivation most clearly. 'No one ever understood any other person's opinion without knowing the language in which that opinion was expressed,' he wrote in the *Adages*. 'And so what did St. Jerome do, when he had decided to expound Holy

others, since all previous ages have toiled that we might reap
the fruit of their wisdom.' And again, the educated man
'should not confine his study to logic, but have a theoretical
acquaintance with all the topics of philosophy ... It is also
desirable that he should not be ignorant of natural philosophy
... nor, while he is acquainted with the divine order of nature,
would I have him ignorant of human affairs. He should
understand the civil law ... he should also be acquainted
with the history of events of past ages..., to be ignorant of
what occurred before you were born is to remain always a
child. For what is the worth of human life, unless it is woven
into the life of our ancestors by the records of history?'

The significance of these passages is that they are taken
respectively from Quintilian's and Cicero's treatises on
oratory. That they *could* have been written in 1500 shows how
firmly the humanistic ideal had seized on the classical notion
that the rhetorician should be able to speak with knowledge,
and in suitable terms, on a wide variety of subjects, broadening the narrowly conceived rhetoric of the *trivium* into a
sort of container for education as a whole.

The fame of the concept of *l'uomo universale* owes much
to its most famous exemplar, Leonardo da Vinci, and its most
eloquent exponent, Castiglione. It was not a new idea. It
was indeed in direct conflict with many humanists' own urge
to study particular branches of learning in depth, acquiring
laborious linguistic skills as they went. In study, in business,
in administration, the drift of the period, indeed the urgent
need of the period, was towards specialisation. For most men,
anything even approaching universal knowledge was attain-
ably only at the level of encylopedism or dilettantism, however attractively Castiglione glossed over the fact. Even at the
level of dilettantism the ideal of universalism was attainable
only by the leisured rich, and it was in this fact that much of
universalism's appeal lay, because it distinguished the gentleman, who did not have to rely for an income on specialised knowledge or skills, from the scholar or craftsman who
did.

The humanists' stress on understanding rather than memory,

divinity was so unpopular with his colleagues that he was compelled to move on to the more sympathetic atmosphere of Alcalà. In spite of the presence of men of a humanistic stamp like Robert Gaguin the Sorbonne remained imperturbably under the influence of its conservative faculty of theology. Oxford and Cambridge were dominated by unyielding faculties of theology, and their resistance to change was made easier by the existence of the Inns of Court which drew off the sons of influential families who, with diplomatic or administrative careers in mind, wanted a more down to earth education.

Even though the chancellor of Cambridge from 1503 was John Fisher, a patron of Erasmus, the university only obtained one lecturer in Greek. At Oxford humanism made more progress, but here it was by means of a new college, Corpus Christi, grafted on to the university by Bishop Richard Fox in 1517. Though founded on a place where, as the statutes put it, 'scholars, like ingenious bees are by day and night to make wax to the honour of God, and honey, dropping sweetness, to the profit of themselves and of all Christians', all its twenty fellows were to be well versed in secular Latin literature. Even more important was the contribution Corpus was to make to the university through a Latin lecturer who was to deal with the poets, orators and historians of ancient Rome, a lecturer in Greek literature and a theology lecturer who was 'as far as possible to follow the ancient and holy doctors both Latin and Greek and especially Jerome, Augustine, Ambrose ... and others of that sort, not Nicholas of Lyra, not Hugh of Vienne and the rest who, as in time so in learning are so far below them.'

Within a year opposition to the 'Greeks' of Corpus had reached such a point that they were set on in the streets by the 'Trojans' of the faculty of theology, and Thomas More was forced to come up from the court and rebuke the university authorities. He defended Fox's intentions by saying that unless theology were to involve a study of the early fathers and of Latin, Greek and Hebrew, it would fall back again into the sterile debates of the schoolmen—that is, continue in its present rut, and he made the point, familiar

Above all, the great majority of books capable of prompting thought and suggesting comparisons and new ideas were still printed in Latin, and were thus inaccessible save to that proportion of the well-educated who had been taught not only to learn Latin but to go on reading it. Individual practice varied. Erasmus wrote only in Latin, Machiavelli only in Italian. Dürer sought advice from Latinists like Pirckheimer when he began to write his treatises in German, and by largely ignoring such advice helped shape German into a language which, as More said of English, 'is plenteous enough to express our minds in anything whereof one man hath used to speak with another.' Yet More wrote *Utopia* in Latin. Yet again, it was Nebrija, a professional humanist who wrote in Latin and edited classical texts, who composed the first grammar of a modern European language and who justified it to Isabella with the famous and prophetic observation that 'language is the perfect instrument of Empire'. Nascent nationalism was indeed one of the factors making for the standardisation and increasing use of the vernacular, though, here again, it was a time of contradiction. Felix Fabri energetically defended German as 'the noblest, most distinguished, most humane of tongues', but his defence was couched in Latin. From the point of view of self-education in humanist ideas, the common reader was to a certain extent a victim of this patriotism, because it led printers to publish national histories and national literature in the vernacular rather than popularise the works of contemporary humanists or translate classical texts. By 1520 the vernacular had still not gained general acceptance as a medium for expressing those aspects of humanism which could have given middle class Europe something like a common culture, and for many who could read Latin but for whom it retained the artificial flavour of a second and unrelished tongue, the ancient world remained alien in its ideas as well as in time.

the censorship of books, why the tremendous reaffirmation of medieval doctrinal accretions by the Council of Trent?

The failure of this approach had little to do with the mild tincture of paganism which accompanied the study of antiquity. Though individual humanists differed in the extent to which they were prepared to bring classical authors into the Christian fold, as it were, without creating a disturbance there—Erasmus being more permissive than Lefèvre and Lefèvre than Colet, for instance—Erasmus spoke for the majority of his fellows when he remarked that 'surely the first place is due to holy scripture; but sometimes I find some things written by the ancieints, by pagans and poets, so chaste, so holy, so divine, that I am persuaded a good genius enlightened them. Certainly there are many in the communion of saints who are not in our catalogue of saints.'

In a sense midway between playful and serious, certain humanists did see themselves as living in the context of ancient manners. Celtis commissioned Hans Burgkmair to anticipate his death in an engraving copied from a Roman tomb, where he lies in the sleep of death mourned by Apollo and Mercury. The tomb of two humanist doctors of medicine, Girolamo and Marcantonio della Torre went as far as to show them being ferried across the Styx towards the Elysian Fields. But classical inconography had become a fairly widespread fashion. The tomb of the two young children of Charles VIII and Anne of France bore scenes from the labours of Hercules in parallel with scenes from the life of Samson, and on Pollaiuolo's monument to Pope Sixtus IV Theology itself was portrayed in the guise of a nude Diana. In 1503 Paolo Cortese, secretary to Pope Alexander VI, published a *Compendium of Dogma* in which the Virgin was called the mother of the Gods, the souls of the dead were referred to as *manes*, Hell was provided with the rivers of the pagan Tartarus, and Aquinas was termed the Apollo of Christianity. When Leo X, patron of humanist learning and as great a collector of classical manuscripts as his fifteenth century forbears, Cosimo *pater patriae* and Lorenzo the Magnificent, entered Rome, it was through arches decorated

it. Christianity became less readily visualisable. The words of Christ became more important than his miracles, even than his crucifixion. Devils, angels, vices, virtues, the cup of the communion held to the blood spurting from Christ's side, Judas hung by the neck, the torture of martyrs—the long heritage of art and drama was belittled by exhortations less to watch and pray than to study and think.

Leading the imagination still further from the liturgy and the subject matter of the pulpit was the surprising eclecticism, the wide variety of source material than humanists thought pertinent to the study of the religious life. One cause was strightforward scholarly curiosity. But there were others: emphasis on moral philosophy, which sought illustrations in poetry, history and rhetoric as well as in scripture; a concern for the very idea of Religion, the impulse to worship traceable in all creeds and at all times; the eclecticism already present in some of the basic humanist models, especially in Cicero.

The sympathetic study of other religions was no longer out of bounds. Each was held to reflect (though Christianity reflected it most directly) a single truth emanating from a single God; from the obelisks of Egypt to the Koran something relevant to God's purposes and man's inherent spirituality was to be found. The risk was that Christianity would not be buttressed but diluted. 'The rites and ceremonies of religion', wrote Cornelius Agrippa, 'are different on account of differences of time and regions; and each religion has something good, which is directed toward God Himself the Creator; and although God approves of the Christian religion alone, yet He does not entirely reject other cults practised for His sake; and He does not leave them wholly unrewarded, if not with eternal, then with a temporal reward; or at least He punishes them less.'

This syncretism was at its most diluting in its reflection of a tendency widely shared among humanists: to combine a refreshingly straightforward approach to the New Testament with an esoterically code-cracking one to the Old. Thus the Jewish Cabala was seen as a corpus of secret lore handed down orally from the time of Moses before being committed to

that God could be worshipped as well in the countryside as in a church; then also the appeal to so many authorities could lead to a distrust of knowledge itself and thus undermine a central tenet of humanism: that by taking thought man could add to his spiritual stature. Burdened by the accumulation of knowledge since the days of Aquinas' reconciliation of reason with faith, oppressed by the number of approaches to the source of belief, it was tempting to pursue knowledge and let faith look after itself. It was tempting to become sceptical —as Pico's nephew Gian Francesco became sceptical—of reason, to see the Philosophy of Christ as essentially a self-contradictory phrase, and, indeed, a despairing one for the men who needed above all the sort of affirmation that only strikes deep enough to give comfort when it is the result of a lightning stroke on the road to Damascus. It was tempting, finally, for the hieroglyph to become confused with the symbols traced in the dust by the magician's staff, and for humanism to lead to man's attempt to ape rather than to seek God, a role into which Agrippa was led and in which he figures as one of the inspirers of Goethe's *Faust*.

Humanism inevitably became involved with religion. Equally inevitably it could act only as a very slow leaven within the spiritual life of Europe as a whole. The humanists wrote in Latin for a relatively, small, if important audience. A few, inside and outside the church, were self-supporting. Some were dependent on the fluctuations of patronage. Others were perched here and there and then not always securely, among universities and other educational institutions. They had no corps of preachers fired with their ideas. They were not involved with the patriotic feelings of any nation to any depth. Above all, perhaps, their message lacked humility and a sense of sin. And because it lacked a sense of sin it lacked the right note of hope. Luther's attitude to theology reflected something of the humanistic tinge which Erfurt university had acquired when he was studying there. In his early years he was an admirer of Erasmus. But one simple passage can explain the breach that developed between the two men and the greater penetrative force of the German's

with human pieces between God and the devil and more in terms of individual ambition, greed and skill, political writers were aware that men's destinies were to some extent within their own control and that this control depended upon self-knowledge. It was useful to limber up by telling the familiar beads of Aristotle's best constitutions and their malign counterparts, but constructive thought could only begin when they were checked against reality. Thus Seyssel had added the pace-making officials, of whatever social background, to the aristocratic element in France's institutional life. Budé, in his very un-Erasmian *Education of a Prince*, pointed out that the nature of a country's economy was more relevant to the political planner than the character of its prince. And Savonarola, brought up on Aquinas' preference for monarchy as the nearest reflection both of God's single rule and that of nature (the queen bee), and anxious as a pastor for a constitution within which men could lead virtuous lives, praised the republican constitution of 1495 both in sermons and in his *Tractate on the government of Florence* because it suited the temperament and rose naturally from the historical conditioning of a particular people.

This emphasis on the workable rather than the ideal was not solely the result of fresh observation. It was aided by medieval and ancient clichés. The body politic was subject to change as the individual body was; it needed the advice of the political diagnostician as the individual needed that of a doctor. Just as the individual was tied to a wheel bearing him from good to ill unless virtue applied the brake, so nations passed from one form of constitution to another, from prosperity to disaster, unless the pressure of knowledge were brought to bear. These metaphors of change had no significance in themselves. No political writer thought the world was slipping into senility, though some preachers and chroniclers did. Outside Italy there was little apprehension about one constitutional form giving way to another: hereditary kingship had been the rule for centuries. But they helped to communicate a sense of urgency and to give a sense of mission to writers. Budé, Seyssel and Machiavelli wrote in the vernacular

Ciceros? Republicans could turn to Livy, monarchists to Suetonius, students of constitutional change to Polybius, idealists to Plato. In itself this plethora of models did not produce works of greater originality than those of the middle ages, let alone works that were more likely to influence those in power; it should, moreover, be remembered that some of what have in retrospect appeared to be key works were not printed until after this period, among them Francesco Guicciardini's *Logrogno Discourse* (1512, printed 1858), Machiavelli's *Prince* (1513, printed 1532) and Budé's *Education of the Prince* (1518 or 1519, printed 1547). But the more sharply classical institutions were seen in terms of their historical development the more apparent it became that all institutions had been made and could be altered by men, and that such alterations had to take into account the tone of society as a whole. The origins and much of the early development of contemporary nations were fogged with myth: those of Rome appeared to be clear. The lack of adequate contemporary reference or analytical books made it easier to see how Roman had been governed than how the larger nations were at the moment, not always excluding a writer's own.

Outside the republics, it was the clarity with which Imperial Rome could be seen that most influenced writers on politics. In Germany, which actually had an emperor, but a weak one, political thought on a national scale remained aspirational rather than practical. In England the notion that the monarch was under the law and was there to protect as well as direct his people blunted the force of Roman analogy, as did the position of the *cortes* in Spain. In France, however, the scorn felt by nearly all those with a humanist education for the *plebs*, together with the growing effectiveness of the monarchy since the reign of Charles VII, led to the least inhibited citation of the Imperial Roman model.

For Budé, first and foremost a scholar by temperament, the power of the king was absolute. To prove that this was not only true in fact but ought to be true in terms of the nature of the ideal polity, he quoted (indeed amended to his purpose) examples from Roman history, he even went so far

with hardly a qualm. When thinking in terms of Florence itself, Machiavelli was bound, and was delighted to be bound, by the traditions of its republican past; he thought in terms of social fairness, of mutual trust, the common good. But when he was thinking of the qualities needed in a leader who was bent on conquest or dealing with conquered territories or negotiating with potential enemies, he accepted the need to dissemble and lie. He expressed a distrust of human nature with more trenchancy than did most of his contemporaries, he pointed to the need for a divorce between private and political morality with more relish, but his views were not isolated. 'Because men are by nature corrupt', wrote Seyssel, 'commonly so ambitious and covetous of dominion . . . that one can put neither trust nor faith in them, it is most suitable and necessary that all princes responsible for the government of realms always keep a wary eye on their neighbours even in time of peace.' Budé sanctioned deceit, bribery and cunning in the national interest. It was not with Machiavelli in mind (of whom he had never heard) that Erasmus reminded his own ideal Christian prince that 'the ways of some princes have slipped back to such a point that the two ideas of "good man" and "prince" seem to be the very antithesis of one another. It is obviously considered foolish and ridiculous to mention a good man in speaking of a prince.'

This, the most 'realistic' aspect of contemporary political thought certainly owed much to the study of antiquity. It was not only that war as such played so prominent a part in the works of Roman historians that it was argued that war was *par excellence* the true subject matter of history, but that writers who paid taxes, knew wars to be expensive and were not born into a fighting caste sympathised with Vegetius' urging that almost any way of defeating an enemy was better than actually fighting him. The concept of Fortune was common to intellectuals. Vegetius, in his widely read *De re militari*, had drawn attention to the dominant role played by fortune on the battlefield. It was reasonable then to endorse the use of terror, deceit and subterfuge—sleights and policies anthologised by another widely read classical author, Fron-

advances that had already been achieved in the natural philosophy taught in the medieval curriculum, while their predominant interest in human behaviour, as studied in relation to classical literature, led them away from the study of nature itself. In universities untouched, or scarcely influenced by humanism, science fared no better; the teaching of natural philosophy had become largely a matter of rote.

And if little was passed down from the universities that encouraged the scientific mood of observation-experiment-hypothesis-new experiment, little was passed up from the trial and error level of technology and craft. Just as there was no 'science' in the sense of a method of investigating natural phenomena which could be transferred, in however diluted a form, to other activities, there was no notion of 'technology' as implying the possibility of increased efficiency or the progressive control by man of his environment. Technological literature (how to paint, cast guns or distil liquors) contained hints that improved methods would enable the next generation to make further progress, but advances in particular arts and crafts did not blend into a general concept of technological progress; that was still inhibited by secrecy and craft exclusiveness. There were occupations where scholars with scientific interest co-operated with skilled and literate artisans. Painters learned anatomy with the aid of surgeons, medical literature benefited from the anatomical drawings and engravings provided by artists, surveyors and the makers of navigational instruments were assisted by mathematicians. Yet these contacts were too isolated and too rare to bring about any general cross-fertilisation between those who thought and those who did. Outside the arts, moreover, there was no welcoming place in contemporary social thought for the artisan with intellectual pretensions, and within the arts intellectual improvement, influenced by the desire to rise from craft status, led to some denigration of the manual element. Leonardo's scorn for the sweaty sculptor was paralleled by the university lecturers in medicine who left dissection to assistants plying the humble trade of surgeon.

a stool, which stool stood upon a bolster of a bed, so tyckle that any man or beast might not touch it so little but it was ready to fall, whereby we perceived that it was not possible that Hun might hand himself the stool so standing ... Also it was not possible that the soft silken girdle should break his neck or skin beneath the girdle. Also we find in a corner somewhat beyond the place where he did hang, a great persell of blood, also we find that upon the left side of Hun's jacket from the breast downward two great streams of blood. Also within the flap of the left side of his jacket we find a great cluster of blood, and the jacket folden down thereupon, which thing the said Hun could never fold nor do after he was hanged. Whereby it appeareth plainly to us all that the neck of Hun was broken, and the great plenty of blood was shed before he was hanged. Wherefore all we find by God and all our consciences that Richard Hun was murdered: also we acquit the said Richard Hun of his own death. Also an end of wax candle which as John Bellringer sayeth he left in the prison burning with Hun that same Sunday at night that Hun was murdered, which wax candle we found sticking upon the stocks fair put out, about seven or eight foot from the place where Hun was hanged, which candle after our opinion was never put out by him, for many likelihoods which we have perceived.*

That curiosity, critical judgement and commonsense did not unite to question received opinions about the nature of the universe is not surprising. The natural philosophers of the twelfth and thirteenth centuries had worked out a vision which embraced all creation from plants and stones to the outermost sphere of the fixed stars which was logical, beautiful and had the sanction of the church. It did not quite explain some of the movements of the heavenly bodies noticed by astronomers. It left room for debate on, say, the nature of motion or the influence of the planets on human behaviour.

* C. H. Williams, ed., *English historical documents*, vol. V, 1485–558 (1967) 660–1.

slaughtered with a copious cheap literature of prognostication in mind. To shift the earth from the centre of the universe would be to upset the calculations of all those who foretold the future or chose auspicious times of the day or month.

Belief in astrology was accompanied by a good deal of mockery. A king of France, so one story ran, went hunting in the expectation of enjoying the fine weather promised by his astrologer. Taking no notice of a miller who warned him that he knew from the horse-flies clustering round his donkey that it would rain, the king rode on into a drenching storm. The casting of horoscopes was actually forbidden by canon law because it denied the concept of free will, but by adopting the formula that the planets 'inclined without constraining' astrologers continued to ply their trade. The influence of humanism led on the whole to an enhanced respect for astrology. The attitude of Cicero was in doubt, but Virgil, Pliny and Ptolemy all appeared to have believed in the power of planetary and sidereal emanations, as did the Plato of the *Timaeus*.

Pico della Mirandola, the firmest opponent of astrology, believed that the planets were thought to be powerful simply because they bore the names of gods who had once been thought to influence men's lives. His attack ranged widely. After keeping a weather diary he found that astrological predictions were correct for only seven out of one hundred and thirty days. If astrology were a science, he asked, why could astrologers never agree among themselves? Astrologers relied on tables of heavenly movements, yet these were known to be erroneous. His key arguments, however, were not based on commonsense observations of this sort, but on his conviction that God had given man the ability to choose his own destiny. How could the planets, mere lumps of rock with pagan names, affect this choice offered to man's spirit? But Pico's attack stood alone because it was based on an intensely personal vision rather than on a chain of verifiable reasoning that reached all the way from keeping his weather diary to wishing to strip the stars of their occult powers. Even Ficino, his older associate, did not deny these powers,

of the age. Pure science lay becalmed among the natural philosophy faculties of the universities. Applied science, the desire to use a knowledge of physical laws to change the environment and improve the quality of life for the individual, was more vigorous, but it was chiefly a matter of horoscopes and spells. As for experiment, it was chiefly amid the retorts and furnaces of the alchemist that inquiring men did not think it demeaning to pour acids and shovel fuel in order to break the secrets of nature.

Apart from a few men of genius, natural philosophy had long been looked upon as something to learn from a handful of near-sacred texts. Once absorbed, so great was the respect for written authorities that the knowledge gleaned became an end in itself, perhaps calling for comment but not prompting further inquiry. And by multiplying authorities humanism had intensified this attitude. Even Copernicus was more concerned to adjust Ptolemy to his theories than to make the ancient authorities obsolete. Moreover, buttressing this respect was a readiness to believe that something became true by being written down. Fostered by the rarity and value of manuscripts, this trait was transferred to the wide public who could now buy printed books. Printing, of course, extended scientific knowledge, but at the same time it spread errors and slowed speculation. By 1500 some three thousand different books dealing with scientific subjects had been published, bringing to the surface not only classical texts of fundamental importance, like Galen's anatomical work *On the Use of the Parts*, but the largely erroneous *Chirurgia* of Guy de Chauliac, thirteenth-century commentaries on Sacrobosco's *Sphere*, and numerous popular compilations purporting to distil all that needed to be known about, say, geometry or physiology in a few pages. Later in the sixteenth century, when the chaff had been winnowed out of this heap, printing would serve science by reporting up-to-date findings and, largely through the use of illustrations, by standardising the way in which these findings were discussed. For the moment, however, the need to absorb overwhelmed the desire to observe, speculate and attempt to prove by experiment.

what Marineo went on to say about them has nothing to do with the scalpel and is entirely characteristic of most of the scientific thought of the period: 'They should understand music, of course, and mathematical training, and whatever pertains to number and to measure, and the causes, motions, influence, nature and effect of the stars; for if a doctor is ignorant of these things he is able neither to diagnose nor to heal.' For the most part 'scientific' enquiry floated uneasily in the void between common-sense observation and an uncritically accepted cosmology.

800,000, elective monarchy. *Norway:* population unknown, hereditary monarchy. In theory, since the union of Kalmar (1397) the Scandinavian kingdoms were governed jointly; in practice Norway followed a course of her own as did Denmark, economically the strongest (controlling the Kattegat through its possession of Bohus, Halland and Scania), while Sweden was divided between an independence and a pro-Danish party. *Italy:* a term whose significance was chiefly geographical but which, in moments of political crisis or cultural debate could refer to a more-or-less common linguistic background and a sense of common origins in Roman antiquity shared by (to name the chief independent powers of the peninsula): *Venice:* population one and a half million, a republic and the only Italian state with an overseas empire, comprising part of Dalmatia, Corfu, Crete, Cyprus and some scattered colonies in southern Greece. *Milan:* population one and a quarter million, a duchy (in 1500, occupied and administered by the French). *Florence:* population three-quarters of a million, republic. *Papal States:* population two millions, elective ecclesiastical principality ruled by the pope. *Naples:* population two millions, hereditary monarchy. Among the smaller independent Italian states were the republics of *Genoa* (which had an uncertain control over Corsica), *Lucca* and *Siena,* the duchies of *Ferrarra, Modena* and *Urbino* and the marquisate of *Mantua. Sicily:* population unknown, hereditary kingdom but dependent upon Aragon. *Spain:* comprising *Aragon,* population one million and *Castile,* population six and a half millions, both hereditary monarchies but ruled jointly by Ferdinand and Isabella, their respective sovereigns, since his sucession in 1479, *Portugal:* population one million, hereditary monarchy. *Navarre:* population unknown, hereditary monarchy. *France:* population nineteen millions, hereditary monarchy. *England:* population three millions, hereditary monarchy. This does not exhaust the list of political entities which operated as independent states either by right, as in the case of the kingdom of *Scotland* and the duchy of *Savoy* or because their nominal superiors were unable to control them, as was the case with certain Baltic cities, like Lübeck and the

# MAPS

FINLAND

RUSSIA

Aland
Island

Gulf of Finland

Novgorod

Stockholm

ESTONIA

Gotland
(to
Denmark)

Pskov

LIVONIA PSKOV

TEUTONIC ORDER

Moscow

Oland

COURLAND

Baltic Sea

Dantzig

TEUTONIC
ORDER

PRUSSIA

NIA

URG

LITHUANIA

SIA

POLAND

VOLHYNIA

Kiev

MORAVIA

Cracow

GALICIA

UKRAINE

IA

PODOLIA

KHANATE OF CRIMEA

TRIA

Vienna

TRANSYLVANIA

BESSARABIA

Sea of
Azov

Buda

MOLDAVIA

HIA

HUNGARY

OLA

WALLACHIA

Black Sea

BOSNIA

SERBIA

HERZEGOVINA

MONTENEGRO

OTTOMAN

Constantinople

Adriatic Sea

RUMELIA

Sea of Marmara

NAPLES

ANATOLIA

EMPIRE

KERMIAN

Corfu

KARAMAN

Aegean
Sea

AIDIN

HAMID

CILICIA

Ionian
Islands

Chios

MENTESHE

TEKKE

MOREA

Naxos

Cerigo

Knights of
St. John

Rhodes

Cyprus

Crete

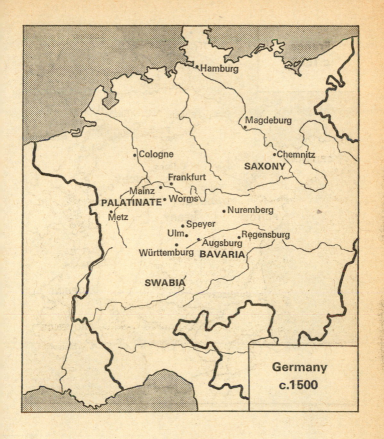

Germany
c.1500

Spain
c.1500

ally on the following works (they are not listed elsewhere in this bibliography).

Beatis, Antonio de. *Die Reise des Kardinals Luigi d'Aragona (1517–1518)* ed. Ludwig Pastor (Freiburg im Breisgau, 1905). he text is in Italian. I quote from my forthcoming translation for the Hakluyt Society.

Castiglione, Baldassare. *The book of the courtier*, tr. George Bull (1967).

Chêrot, M. 'La société au commencement du XVI<sup>e</sup> siècle (d'après les homélies de Josse Clichtove) 1472–1543', *Revue des Questions Historiques* (1895).

Coquillart, Guillaume. *Oeuvres* (2 vols., Paris, 1857).

Crotch, W. J. B., ed. *The prologues and epilogues of William Caxton* (1928).

La Borderie, A. de. *Oeuvres françaises d'Olivier Maillard: sermons et poésies* (Nantes, 1877).

Landucci, Luca. *A Florentine diary from 1450 to 1516*, tr. Alice de Rosen Jervis (1927).

Lynn, Caro. *A college professor of the Renaissance* [Marineo Siculo] (Chicago, 1937).

More, Sir Thomas. *Utopia*, in *The complete works of St. Thomas More*, vol. 4, ed. Edward Surtz and J. H. Hexter (Yale, 1965).

Nauert, Charles G. *Agrippa and the crisis of Renaissance thought* (University of Illinois, 1965).

Nève, Joseph. *Sermons choisis de Michel Menot, 1508–1518* (Paris, 1924).

Oulmont, Charles. *La poésie morale, politique et dramatique à le veille de la Renaissance: Pierre Gringore* (Paris, 1910).

Panofsky, Erwin. *The life and art of Albrecht Dürer* (Princeton, 1955).

Phillips, Margaret Mann. *The 'Adages' of Erasmus* (Cambridge U.P., 1964).

Rojas, Fernando de, *The Spanish Bawd* (*La Celestina*), tr. J. H. Cohen (1964).

Seyssel, Claude de. *La monarchie de France*, ed. J. Poujol (Paris, 1961).

Speroni, Charles. *Wit and wisdom of the Italian Renaissance* (U. of California, 1964).

Spitz, Lewis W. *Conrad Celtis, the German arch-humanist* (Harvard U.P., 1957).

*Portuguese seaborne empire, 1415–1825* (1969); C. O. Sauer, *The early Spanish Main* (U. of California, 1966); R. H. Major, tr. and ed., *Christopher Columbus, four voyages to the New World: letters and selected documents* (Reprint, N.Y., 1961); E. G. Ravenstein, ed., *The journal of the first voyage of Vasco da Gama, 1497–1499* (Hakluyt Soc., 1898); W. B. Greenlee, tr. and ed., *The voyage of Pedro Alvares Cabral to Brazil and India* (Hakluyt Soc., 1938); Lodovico di Varthema, *The Travels,* tr. J. W. Jones, ed. G. P. Badger (Hakluyt Soc., 1863).

## POLITICAL EUROPE

General discussions: G. R. Potter, 'The beginnings of the modern state', *History* (1946) 73–84; Garrett Mattingly, 'Changing attitudes toward the state during the Renaissance', in *Facets of the Renaissance,* ed. W. H. Werkmeister (N.Y., 1959); Gerhardt Ritter, 'Origins of the modern state', and Federico Chabod, 'Was there a Renaissance State?' in Heinz Lubasz, ed., *The development of the modern state* (N.Y., 1964). On propaganda: G. E. Waas, *The legendary character of the Kaiser Maximilian* (N.Y., 1914); J. Chartrou, *Les entrées solonelles et trionphales à la Renaissance 1484–1551* (Paris, 1928); Sydney Anglo, *Spectacle, pageantry and early Tudor policy* (Oxford, 1969); L. D. Ettlinger, *The Sistine Chapel before Michelangelo: religious imagery and papal primacy* (Oxford, 1965). Individual countries: George Vernadsky, *Russia at the dawn of the modern age* (Yale U.P., 1959); J. L. I. Fennell, *Ivan the Great of Moscow* (1961); Ian Grey, *Ivan III and the unification of Russia* (1964); J. H. Elliott, *Imperial Spain, 1469–1716* (1963); John Lynch, *Spain under the Habsburgs,* vol. i (Oxford, 1964); H. S. Offler, 'Aspects of government in the late medieval empire', in *Europe in the late Middle Ages,* ed. J. R. Hale, J. R. C. Highfield and B. Smalley (1965); Hans Baron, 'Imperial reform and the Habsburgs, 1486–1504: a new interpretation', *American Historical Review* (October, 1939) 293–303; H. J. Cohn, *The government of the Rhine Palatinate in the fifteenth century* (Oxford U.P., 1965); P. S. Lewis, *Later Medieval France* (1968); R. Mousnier, *Études sur la France de 1494 à 1559* (Cours de Sorbonne, Paris, n.d.); R. Russell Major, *Representative institutions in Renaissance France* (Madison, 1960); Denys Hay, *The Italian Renaissance in its historical setting* (Cambridge U.P., 1961); Nicolai Rubinstein,

de frontière', in *International Commission of Historical Sciences*, Bulletin, vol. v (Warsaw, 1933) 540–59; Denys Hay, *Europe: the emergence of an idea* (Edinburgh U.P., 1957); W. H. McNeill, *Europe's steppe frontier* (Chicago U.P., 1964); A. S. Atiya, *The crusade in the later Middle Ages* (1938). Life outside the Towns: Yvonne Bézard, *La vie rurale dans le sud de la région Parisienne de 1450 à 1550* (Paris, 1929); W. G. Hoskins, *Provincial England* (1963); and inside the towns: Gerald Strauss—a book I have drawn on heavily—*Nuremberg in the sixteenth century* (N.Y., 1966); Bartolomé Bennassar, *Valladolid au siècle d'or: une ville de Castille et sa campagne au XVIᵉ siècle* (Paris, 1967); J. B. Wadsworth, *Lyons 1473–1503, The beginnings of cosmopolitanism* (Cambridge, Mass., 1962), and Lucien Romier, 'Lyons and cosmopolitanism at the beginning of the French Renaissance', in Werner L. Gundersheimer, ed., *French humanism 1470–1600* (1969); Miriam U. Chrisman, *Strasbourg and the reform: a study in the process of change* (Yale U.P., 1967); and Jacques Heers, *Genes au XVᵉ siècle* (Paris, 1901).


ECONOMIC EUROPE

E. E. Rich and C. H. Wilson, eds., *The Cambridge economic history of Europe*, vol. iv (Cambridge U.P., 1967); Philippe Dollinger, *La Hanse, XIIᵉ–XVIIᵉ siècles* (Paris, 1964); Richard Ehrenberg, *Capital and finance in the age of the Renaissance*, tr. H. M. Lucas (1928); Raymond de Roover, *The rise and decline of the Medici Bank, 1397–1494* (Harvard U.P., 1963); Gertrude R. B. Richards, *Florentine merchants in the age of the Medici* (Harvard U.P., 1932); M. Bresnard, *Les foires de Lyon au XVᵉ et XVIᵉ siècles* (Paris, 1924); Jean-François Bergier, *Genève et l'économie Européenne de la Renaissance* (Paris, 1903); Jean Delumeau, *L'alun de Rome, XVᵉ–XVIᵉ siècles* (Paris, 1962); F. C. Lane, *Venetian ships and shipbuilders* (Baltimore, 1934) and *Venice and history: the collected papers of F.C. Lane* (Baltimore, 1966); Julius Klein, *The Mesta: a study in Spanish economic history* (Harvard U.P., 1920); Joan Thirsk, ed., *The agrarian history of England and Wales*, vol. iv (Cambridge U.P., 1967); Lawrence Stone, 'State control in sixteenth-century England', *Economic History Review* (1947) 103–20. And see *Class*, 'In the towns'.

(1955) 321–66. In the towns: Jean V. Alter, *Les origines de la satire anti-Bourgeoise en France. Moyen age—XVIᵉ siècle* (Geneva, 1966); P. Boissonade, *Le socialisme d'état. L'industrie et les classes industrielles en France pendant les deux premiers siècles de l'ère moderne, 1453–1661* (Paris, 1927); L. Febvre, 'Types économiques et sociaux du XVIᵉ siècle: le marchand', *Revue des Cours et Conférences* (1921) 57–65, 143–57; Régine Pernoud, *Histoire de la bourgeoisie en France*, vol. i (Paris, 1960); Emile Coornaert, *Les corporations en France avant 1789* (Paris, 1941); Sylvia Thrupp, *The merchant class of medieval London*, 1300–1500 (Chicago U.P., 1948); J. A. Goris, *Études sur les colonies marchands méridionales à Anvers, 1488–1567* (Louvain, 1925); J. H. Hexter, 'The education of the aristocracy in the Renaissance', in his *Reappraisals in history* (1961).

## RELIGION

General: R. Aubenas and Ricard, *L'église et la Renaissance, 1449–1517* (Paris, 1951); Pierre Imbart de la Tour, *Les origines de la Réforme*, vol. i (Paris, 1905); Lucien Febvre, *Au coeur religieux du XVIᵉ siècle* (Paris, 1957); P. S. Allen, *The Age of Erasmus* (Oxford U.P., 1914); H. A. Enno van Gelder, *The two Reformations of the sixteenth century. A study of the religious aspects and consequences of the Renaissance and humanism* (The Hague, 1961); J. Toussaert, *Le sentiment religieux en Flandre à la fin du moyen-age* (Paris, 1960). Church and state: R. J. Knecht, 'The Concordat of 1516', *University of Birmingham Historical Journal* (1963) 16–32; Henry Kamen, *The Spanish Inquisition* (1965). Clerics: Ludwig Pastor, *The History of the Popes*, vols. iv–viii, tr. F. I. Antrobus (1894 seq.); M. E. Mallett, *The Borgias* (1969); D. S. Chambers, 'The economic predicament of Renaissance cardinals', in *Studies in Medieval and Renaissance History*, vol. iii (U. of Nebraska, 1966); David Knowles, *The religious orders in England*, vol. iii (Cambridge U.P., 1961); Margaret Bowker, *The secular clergy in the diocese of Lincoln, 1450–1520* (Cambridge U.P., 1968). Church and people: Emile Mâle, *L'art religieux de la fin du moyen âge en France* (Paris, 1925); Mirella Levi d'Ancona, *The iconography of the Immaculate Conception in the Middle Ages and early Renaissance* (College Art Association of America, 1957); D. Weinstein, 'Savonarola, Florence, and the

Cohen, *Le théatre en France au moyen age* (2 vols. Paris, 1928, 1931), and *Histoire de la mise en scène dans le théatre religieux français du moyen age* (Paris, 1926); Jean Jacquot, ed., *Le lieu théatrale à la Renaissance* (Paris, 1964); H. G. Harvey, *Theatre of the Bazoche* (Harvard U.P., 1941); E. K. Chambers, *The medieval stage*, vol. ii (Oxford U.P., 1903); Glynne Wickham, *Early English Stages 1300 to 1600*, vol. I (1959); Douglas Radcliffe-Umsted, *The birth of modern comedy in Renaissance Italy* (Chicago University Press, 1969); G. R. Kernodle, *From art to theatre: form and convention in the Renaissance* (Chicago U.P., 1944). Fine Arts: Elizabeth G. Holt, ed., *A documentary history of art*, vol. i (N.Y., 1957); John White, *The birth and rebirth of pictorial space* (1957); E. H. Gombrich, 'The Renaissance theory of art and the rise of landscape', in his *Norm and Form* (1966); Anthony Blunt, *Artistic theory in Italy 1450–1600* (Oxford U.P., 1940); J. Jex-Blake and E. Sellers, *The Elder Pliny's chapter on the history of art* (1896); Otto Benesch, *The art of the Renaissance in Northern Europe* (rev. ed., 1965); Charles de Tolnay, *Hieronymus Bosch* (1966; Charles Garside, *Zwingli and the arts* (Yale U.P., 1966); Wolfgang Stechow, *Northern Renaissance art 1400–1600* (Englewood Cliffs, N. J., 1966); Anthony Blunt, *Art and architecture in France 1500–1700* (1953); Albert Châtelet and Jacques Thuillier, *La peinture française du Fouquet à Poussin* (Geneva, 1963); Lawrence Stone, *Sculpture in Britain: The Middle Ages* (1955); André Chastel, *The Golden Age of the Renaissance: Italy 1460–1500*, tr. J. Griffin (1965), *The studios and styles of the Renaissance: Italy 1460–1500*, tr. J. Griffin (1966) and *Art et humanisme à Florence au temps de Laurent le Magnifique* (Paris, 1960); R. Klein and H. Zerner, *Italian Art 1500–1600* (Englewood Cliffs, N.J., 1960); Eve Borsook, *The mural painters of Tuscany* (1960); John Shearman, *Andrea del Sarto* (2 vols. Oxford U.P., 1965); Edgar Wind, *Bellini's Feast of the Gods* (Harvard U.P., 1948); John Pope-Hennessy, *The portrait in the Renaissance* (1967), *Italian Renaissance sculpture* (1958), and 'The Italian Plaquette', *Proceedings of the British Academy* (1964) 63–85.

SECULAR LEARNING

Humanism: R. R. Bolgar, *The classical inheritance* (Cambridge U.P., 1952); Robert Weiss, *The Renaissance discovery of classical antiquity* (Oxford, 1969); P. O. Kristeller, *The Classics and*

Philippe de Comines, *Mémoirs*, (Paris, 1925). Science: Edgar Zilsel, 'The genesis of the concept of scientific progress', in *Roots of scientific thought*, ed. P. P. Wiener and Aaron Noland (N.Y., 1957); Marie Boas, *The Scientific Renaissance, 1450–1630* (1962); George Sarton, *Six Wings: men of science in the Renaissance* (1958); B. Gille, *Les ingénieurs de la Renaissance* (Paris, 1964); Margaret T. Hodgen, *Early anthropology in the sixteenth and seventeenth centuries* (U. of Pennsylvania, 1964); Giorgio de Santillana, 'The Role of art in the Scientific Renaissance', in *The Rise of Science in Relation to Society*, ed. L. M. Marsak (1964); Joan Gadol, 'The unity of the Renaissance: humanism, natural science and art', in *From the Renaissance to the Counter-Reformation: essays in honour of Garrett Mattingly*, ed. Charles H. Carter (1966).

# INDEX

Administration, 79 *et seq.*, 96, 104 *et seq.*

age (civil and personal), 15, 16–18

Agricola, Rudolph, 248

Agrippa, Cornelius, 115, 122, 128, 171, 301, 304

Alamanni, Lodovico, 214

Albert of Brandenburg, Archbishop of Mainz, 224, 225

Alberti, Leon Battista, 269

Albuquerque, Affonso d', 139

Aldus (Aldus Manutius), 189

Alexander VI, Pope, 16, 18, 72, 92, 101, 220, 225, 227, 228, 237, 299

Alfonso, Prince of Portugal, 94

Altdorfer, Albrecht, 45

Alvares, Francisco, 186

Alviano, Bartolomeo, 314

Amboise, Georges, Cardinal d', 69, 87, 224

Anne of Brittany, Queen of France, 15, 67, 94, 127

Aquinas, St. Thomas, 233, 287, 290, 299, 303, 305

Aragon, Beatrice, of 37

Aragon, Cardinal of, 14

Aragon, Catherine of, *see* Catherine

Aragon, Ferdinand of, *see* Ferdinand

architecture, 273–4

Ariosto, Lodovico, 214, 256, 282

aristocracy, 96, 198, 210–15

Aristotle, 146, 168, 248, 275, 286, 292, 298, 305, 314

Arminius, 110, 111

Art (The Arts), 246–74, *see* also architecture, drama, music, painting and sculpture

Arthur, Prince of Wales, 75, 76, 94, 296

astrology, 183, 314–16

astronomy, 313–14

Augustine, St., 233

Autun, Jean d', 24

Balboa, Vasco Nuñez de, 47

Baldovinerti Alessio, 45

banditry, 26, 33

banking, 138, 146 *et seq.*, 152

Barbari, Jacopo de, 262

Barbaro, Emolao, 290

Barclay, Alexander, 113, 176, 184

Bartolommeo, Fra, 187, 273

Bavaria, Dukes Ludwig and Wilhelm of, 82

Bayard, Pierre, Seigneur de, 192

Bayezid II, Sultan of Turkey, 103

Beatis, Antonio de, 13, 132, 266, 270

Beaune, Jacques de, 151, 182

Bellini, Giovanni, 132, 266, 270

Bembo, Pietro, 46, 182

Benedetto da Maino, 277

Bernaldez, Andres, 195

Bernardino of Feltre, Fra, 194

Bertoldo di Giovanni, 102

Bibbiena, Bernardo Dovizi, 256

Bisticci, Vespasiano da, 127, 190

Boiardo, Matteo Maria, 214

Boccaccio, Giovanni, 44, 256

Bohemian Brethen, 91, 242

Borgia, Cesare, 29, 65, 126

Borgia, Lucrezia, 115

Borgia, Rodrigo, *see* Alexander VI

Bosch, Hieronymus, 265

# The Fontana History of Europe

**Renaissance Europe 1480–1520**   J. R. Hale
The latest addition to the series.

**Reformation Europe 1517–1559**   G. R. Elton
'Not since Ranke has any historian described the religious and
political history of Central Europe during the Reformation with as
much insight and authority.'                                    *History*

**Europe Divided 1559–1598**   J. H. Elliott
'John Elliott is no ordinary historian. He writes without fuss, but
with a sure instinct for words; he is always in command of his
material; always unprejudiced but never unfeeling. He is scru-
pulously fair in his tight allocation of space, and on every subject
he commands confidence and respect.'   *J. P. Kenyon, The Observer*

**Europe Unfolding 1648–1688**   John Stoye
'A survey which is the best of its kind available in any language.'
*The Times Literary Supplement*

**Europe of the Ancien Régime 1715–1783**   David Ogg
'An excellent introduction to eighteenth-century Europe.'
*The Times Literary Supplement*

**Revolutionary Europe 1783–1815**   George Rudé
'A thoughtful and thought-provoking book. There have been many
reflections on the French Revolution since Burke's but few have
been as unprejudiced or as wise as Professor Rudé's.'   *The Economist*

**Europe Between Revolutions 1815–1848**   Jacques Droz
A translation of a work by a distinguished French historian,
specially commissioned for the series.

**Europe of the Dictators 1919–1945**   Elizabeth Wiskemann
'A model of succinctness and clarity.' *G. L. Mosse, Journal of
Contemporary History*

*In preparation*: volumes by J. A. S. Grenville, F. H. Hinsley and
Hugh Trevor-Roper.